ENCOUNTERING

JESUS

in Word, Sacraments, and Works of Charity

PETER J. VAGHI

author of the Pillars of Faith series

ave maria press  notre dame, indiana

Nihil Obstat: Rev. Michael Heintz
                  Censor Librorum

Imprimatur: Most Rev. Kevin C. Rhoades
                  Bishop of Fort Wayne-South Bend
                  Given at Fort Wayne, Indiana, on 15 April 2013.

Founded in 1865, Ave Maria Press is a ministry of the United States Province of Holy Cross.

www.avemariapress.com

ISBN-10 1–59471–432–0, ISBN-13 978–1–59471–432–0

E-book ISBN-10 1–59471–433–9, ISBN-13 978–1–59471–433-7

Cover image © Art Resource, Inc.

Cover and text design by David Scholtes.

Printed and bound in the United States of America.

Library of Congress Cataloging-in-Publication Data is available.

Founded in 1865, Ave Maria Press,
a ministry of the Congregation of
Holy Cross, is a Catholic publishing
company that serves the spiritual and
formative needs of the Church and its
schools, institutions, and ministers;
Christian individuals and families; and
others seeking spiritual nourishment.

———◦◉◦———

For a complete listing of titles from

Ave Maria Press

Sorin Books

Forest of Peace

Christian Classics

visit www.avemariapress.com

ave maria press® / Notre Dame, IN 46556
A Ministry of the United States Province of Holy Cross

"A beautiful and thoughtful study . . . out of the heart of a seasoned preacher, successful teacher, and committed evangelizer."

Cardinal Donald Wuerl
Archbishop of Washington

"The New Evangelization tells us that our faith is in a person, Jesus, the Second Person of the Blessed Trinity. Msgr. Peter Vaghi—a precise theologian, a compelling teacher, a good pastor—helps us meet this person as he speaks, as he sacrifices, as he loves."

Cardinal Timothy M. Dolan
Archbishop of New York

"Through his Pillars of Faith series, Msgr. Peter Vaghi has emerged as a master teacher of the faith. His latest book is full of fine insights and practical reflections on making the faith come alive in our lives. This is inspiring reading."

Msgr. Stephen J. Rossetti
Author of *Letters to My Brothers*

"The life of Catholics and, indeed, of all Christians, brings with it a call to encounter Jesus, day by passing day. Msgr. Peter Vaghi vividly illustrates how this encounter takes place through pondering the Gospel stories, receiving the sacraments, and practicing loving service to those in need."

Gerald O'Collins, S.J.
Author of *A Midlife Journey*

"*Encountering Jesus in Word, Sacraments, and Works of Charity* is an invaluable resource for anyone looking to deepen their Catholic faith. In these pages the reader will find clear and rich expositions of the Catholic faith as believed, celebrated, lived, and prayed. Msgr. Vaghi's book is an invitation to continue on your daily path of encountering Christ in his word, sacraments, and through acts of charity so you can become an active participant in the New Evangelization."

Jem Sullivan
Author of *Opening the Door of Faith*

"Here in the Nuba Mountains of Sudan, where death is met daily, Msgr. Vaghi's book has been my retreat into God's mercy and love—a reminder to find him not only in the patients I am blessed to serve, but also each morning when I receive him in the Eucharist."

Sr. Deirdre M. Byrne, P.O.S.C.
Little Worker of the Sacred Hearts

The Pillars of Faith Series
by Peter J. Vaghi

The Faith We Profess:
A Catholic Guide to the Apostles' Creed

The Sacraments We Celebrate:
A Catholic Guide to the Seven Mysteries of Faith

The Commandments We Keep:
A Catholic Guide to Living a Moral Life

The Prayer We Offer:
A Catholic Guide to Communion with God

In grateful memory of my dear father,
Joseph P. Vaghi, Jr. (1920–2012)
May he rest in eternal peace!

Special gratitude to the parishioners of
Little Flower Parish
and members of the John Carroll Society,
to my editor Robert Hamma,
and to Reverend Anthony Lickteig.

Contents

Foreword

The call of the New Evangelization is to deepen our own faith in Jesus and his Gospel, to confirm our confidence in its power to transform the world, and finally to share this Good News with others. This is the vision of the recently concluded 2012 Synod on the New Evangelization for the Transmission of the Christian Faith and the challenge of the Church's perennial mission to bring people to Christ.

Monsignor Peter Vaghi takes the title of his book *Encountering Jesus in Word, Sacraments, and Works of Charity* from Benedict XVI's encyclical letter *God Is Love*. But the text of this inspiring publication begins with an even wider perspective. Jesus entrusted the Church to go out to all nations and share the joy of the Gospel and with this command established evangelization as the mission of the Church (Mt 28:18–20). Pope Paul VI in his apostolic exhortation *Evangelii Nuntiandi* described the Church as "a community which is in its turn evangelizing, meaning that those who have experienced the love of Jesus and live within the Church can and must communicate and spread it" (13).

Following the conclusion of the Second Vatican Council and with the pontificate of Pope Paul VI, the Church began to think about a new expression of Catholic evangelization in response to a rapidly changing world. The New Evangelization opens up a way of seeing a whole range of activities carried on by the Church to spread the Good News. Following the Synod in 2012, we can speak of three aspects of evangelization.

First, "ordinary pastoral ministry must be more animated by the fire of the Spirit." Second, we are called to "proclaim the Gospel to those people who do not know Jesus Christ." Finally, the mission of the New Evangelization is to find new ways to help renew the faith lives of people who have drifted away from the Church so that they may "encounter Jesus Christ anew, rediscover the joy of faith and return to the religious practice in the community of the faithful" (Homily for Closing Mass, Synod of Bishops, October 28, 2012).

Monsignor Vaghi writes that the idea for this book came from Benedict XVI's reflections on the New Evangelization. As a successful pastor with long experience, Monsignor Vaghi has given us an example of the pastoral application of Benedict XVI's vision for more fully engaging the parish and the laity in the mission of the Church.

Encountering Jesus in Word, Sacraments and Works of Charity is a type of formation manual for Catholics who desire to be evangelizers. It invites the reader to take up the practice of meditation on scripture, reflecting on his or her own experience in order to find ways to act on those reflections in personal witness and works of charity. We are asked not just to read about how to encounter the Lord in the Word, but also to take up the Word and find ourselves in the story of Jesus' life and mission.

In this way we discover that evangelization is not a program but rather a way of life. It is a way of living out our baptismal vocation in our family and with our coworkers and neighbors. Catholic evangelizers are helped to realize that the sacraments shape our vision and our approach to evangelization. Our participation in the sacraments is what makes evangelization "Catholic."

Monsignor Vaghi writes that the sacrament of Penance is the "primary sacrament of the New Evangelization." One of the obstacles to evangelization is a "spiritual paralysis that makes us unbending, uncooperative, and unforgiving," rendering us unable to share the joy of living with Jesus. This kind of paralysis can only be healed through reconciliation and in the gift of the sacrament. Evangelization begins with acknowledging that we can always grow deeper in our love for the Lord.

Often, when Catholics are invited to think seriously about the opportunities they have for evangelization, they express great hesitation, thinking they lack knowledge of the faith, or eloquent speech, or confidence. What they sometimes miss is the connection between works of charity and evangelization. Here we think about our Blessed Mother's response to her encounter with the angel Gabriel and conceiving our Lord by the power of the Holy Spirit. Carrying our Lord, she went "in haste" (with a sense of urgency) to visit and help her cousin Elizabeth. Monsignor Vaghi writes, "In works of charity we encounter the Lord in another and in ourselves."

What is true for us as individuals is also true for us as a Church. In this light, our ability to evangelize opens up endless possibilities from an act of kindness for a coworker, to caring lovingly for an aging parent or a sick child, to inviting a friend we know is far from the Lord to Mass.

Encountering Jesus in Word, Sacraments, and Works of Charity is a beautiful and thoughtful study on how to develop the consciousness of an evangelizer and a keen appreciation for the urgency of the New Evangelization. For this reason alone it is a timely contribution to the mission of the Church and therefore to each of us. It is also most welcome because it comes out of the heart of a seasoned preacher, successful teacher, and committed evangelizer.

Cardinal Donald Wuerl
Archbishop of Washington

Introduction

The title of this book, *Encountering Jesus in Word, Sacraments, and Works of Charity*, draws its inspiration from various talks of Benedict XVI. The clear, overarching, and consistent approach of Benedict XVI in his teaching and the direction of his theological vision is an "encounter" with Christ, with God. It is his fundamental way of approaching our relationship with God. In fact, while on the airplane on his way to Germany for his state visit, he said, "Therefore I know that . . . a great many people are waiting for me joyfully, waiting for a celebration of faith, a being together, and they look forward to the joy of *encountering God*."[1]

In the very first paragraph of his first encyclical letter, *Deus Caritas Est* (*God Is Love*), Benedict XVI wrote:

> Being Christian is not the result of an ethical choice or a lofty idea, *but the encounter with an event, a person*, which gives life a new horizon and a decisive direction. . . . Since God has first loved us . . . love is now no longer a mere "command"; it is the response to the gift of love with which God draws near to us. (*DCE* 1; emphasis added)

And that "encounter" of love is with Jesus. That is
the basis of our friendship with him as a follower of
Jesus. It is a personal relationship and an encounter.

In a beautiful homily given at Regensburg,
Germany, in 2006, Benedict XVI spoke of the
Apostles' Creed: "The Creed is not a collection of
propositions; it is not a theory. It is anchored in the
event of Baptism—a genuine encounter between God
and man." For him, the Creed is thus primarily an
encounter with Christ and not just a way of express-
ing the contents of our faith.

In one of his first homilies after his election, as if to
set the tone for his papacy, Benedict XVI said, "There
is nothing more beautiful than to be surprised by the
Gospel, by the encounter with Christ. There is nothing more beautiful than to know Him and to speak to
others of our friendship with Him" (April 24, 2005).

Already, in the early days of Pope Francis, this
theme of an encounter with Jesus Christ seems to
continue:

> Inspired also by the celebration of the Year of
> Faith, all of us together, pastors and members
> of the faithful, will strive to respond faithfully
> to the Church's perennial mission: to bring Je-
> sus Christ to mankind and to lead mankind *to
> an encounter with Jesus Christ, the Way, the Truth,
> and the Life, truly present in the Church and also in
> every person.* This meeting leads us to become
> new men in the mystery of Grace, kindling in the
> spirit that Christian joy that is the hundredfold
> given by Christ to those who welcome him into

their lives. (Address to the College of Cardinals, March 15, 2013; emphasis added)

This book focuses on the three ways to encounter Jesus: in the Word of God, in the sacraments, and in the witness of charity. In *Deus Caritas Est*, Benedict XVI wrote:

> The Church's deepest nature is expressed in her three-fold responsibility: of proclaiming the word of God (*kerygma-martyria*), celebrating the sacraments (*leitourgia*), and exercising the ministry of charity (*diakonia*). These duties presuppose each other and are inseparable. (*DCE* 25)

He stated further, "The Church cannot neglect the service of charity any more than she can neglect the Sacraments and the Word" (*DCE* 22). As the Church is the Body of Christ, the Word, sacraments, and works of charity express the deepest nature of the Church. It is in these three ways that we encounter Jesus in our time.

Part I:
Encountering Jesus
in His Word

ONE

The Making of an Evangelizer

In *Verbum Domini* (Word of the Lord), his 2010 Apostolic Exhortation following the Synod on the Word of God, Benedict XVI wrote, "The Christian life is essentially marked by an encounter with Jesus Christ, who calls us to follow him" (*VD* 72). The first way that we can encounter Jesus is through his Word. It is there that we come to meet and know and be affected by him through our meditative and prayerful appropriation of his holy Word.

In these days and at this time in history, I would suggest that our Church and our world are eagerly awaiting a new encounter with Jesus. Let us look to Peter and his encounter with Jesus. He is a model for you and me on what it means to be an evangelizer for Christ. This is especially true as our Church—at all levels—is becoming committed to a New Evangelization, which challenges each of us to become more faithful and faith-filled evangelizers.

The New Evangelization is the challenge to repropose in new ways the ancient verities of our faith to members of our families, coworkers, fallen-away Catholics, and whomever the Lord puts in our way. The archbishop of Washington, Cardinal Donald Wuerl,

perceptively described the cultural climate of evangelization to the 2012 Synod of Bishops, whose theme
was "The New Evangelization for the Transmission of
the Christian Faith." Speaking of our time, he stated,
"It is as if a tsunami of secular influence has swept
across the cultural landscape, taking with it such soci-
etal markers as marriage, family, the concept of the
common good and objective right and wrong."[2] Such
is the present climate for the New Evangelization.

Peter's encounter with Jesus is informative as we
consider the challenges of the New Evangelization. I
invite you to reflect with me on Luke 5:1–11, the call
of Peter, the fisherman. It is a well-known passage.
Put yourself in the passage as you read.

> While the crowd was pressing in on Jesus and
> listening to the word of God, he was standing by
> the Lake of Gennesaret. He saw two boats there
> alongside the lake; the fishermen had disem-
> barked and were washing their nets. Getting into
> one of the boats, the one belonging to Simon, he
> asked him to put out a short distance from the
> shore. Then he sat down and taught the crowds
> from the boat. After he had finished speaking,
> he said to Simon, "Put out into deep water and
> lower your nets for a catch." Simon said in re-
> ply, "Master, we have worked hard all night and
> have caught nothing, but at your command I
> will lower the nets." When they had done this,
> they caught a great number of fish and their nets
> were tearing. They signaled to their partners in
> the other boat to come to help them. They came

and filled both boats so that they were in danger of sinking. When Simon Peter saw this, he fell at the knees of Jesus and said, "Depart from me, Lord, for I am a sinful man." For astonishment at the catch of fish they had made seized him and all those with him, and likewise James and John, the sons of Zebedee, who were partners of Simon. Jesus said to Simon, "Do not be afraid; from now on you will be catching men." When they brought their boats to the shore, they left everything and followed him. (Lk 5:1–11)

This is a most revealing story, not only about the initial difficulties at catching fish and a sudden turn for the better, but also about Jesus' preaching the Word of God and his preparing Peter and the others to do the same thing—to be evangelizers. The story is full of details and carefully chosen words—a gospel passage from St. Luke that also speaks directly to you and me.

We read that the crowd was "pressing in on Jesus and listening to the word of God." In effect, they encountered him precisely in their listening to the Word of God for he is the Word of God enfleshed. In listening to his Word, they encountered him—as do we.

In addition, each of us can certainly identify with Jesus, who must have been so very tired—for the crowds had been pressing against him all day as he preached the Word of God. We know that feeling! At the end of a long day filled with appointments, phone calls, e-mails, and text messages, sometimes we would just like to disappear from the world. But we know we cannot.

Jesus probably felt the same and wanted to disappear. Instead he got into Peter's boat and asked him to pull out a short way, where Jesus continued to teach the crowds. This time, however, Jesus did it sitting down. Peter encountered him more closely. It shows that Jesus wanted to be with Peter, as he wants to be with us, more closely in the specific, concrete times of our lives.

He chose Peter's boat out of all the boats. Peter must have felt so proud that the Lord had singled him out. Yet Peter certainly could not have had any idea what was in store for him. He could not have known why it was that Jesus had picked his boat and why it was that Jesus, after he had finished speaking, asked Peter to pull out into deep water and lower his net.

In reflecting on this passage, I invite you to focus on two aspects of the text, two aspects that help explain its underlying meaning.

First, consider Peter's response to Jesus: "Master, we have worked hard all night and have caught nothing." The words "worked hard" are used in other places in the New Testament typically to mean "apostolic toil." In other words, we have put in a lot of work, expended much energy, exhausted ourselves, and nothing has come of it. There is a sense of weariness in Peter's choice of words, a certain defeatism and lack of confidence. "Lord, you could have helped us from the beginning, why did you not?"

It was Peter's turn to make a choice. He could have given in to his weariness, telling Jesus that he had already tried. He could have said it is no use or it is better to go home. In effect, he could have simply rejected Jesus' request. That can happen to us when Jesus asks us to make certain decisions in life. We reject his Word and follow our own instincts. But not Peter!

He decided to obey the Word of Jesus. He consciously decided to take a chance, put out into the deep, and lower the nets—to run a small risk, to ignore his overwhelming fatigue and the threat of ridicule among his coworkers and friends.

In effect, he listened to and obeyed the Word of God, the Word of Jesus. Moreover, he trusted in the Word of Jesus. After all, it is precisely the work of Jesus and not primarily our own work. And in the process, he became a changed man.

By his command to put out into the deep, Jesus was forming him to be not only an apostle, an evangelizer, but eventually the leader of the apostles. For sure, we know so well from scripture that Peter would continue to vacillate and even deny Jesus in the garden. He did it not once but three times. But in this text, Jesus was helping Peter to see that obeying and trusting the Word of God can lead to an incredible success. The men caught such a great number of fish that their nets were at the breaking point.

The true evangelizer stands challenged at such moments, whether it is a question of taking a little risk (or even a large risk), throwing himself into something, or not stopping to calculate or weigh things too much.

He is challenged to simply listen to and follow the Word of God. In this case, his Word is simply: "Put out into deep water and lower your nets for a catch." It is a Word full of risks.

So it must be with us. We are challenged to take risks for Jesus even when we seem to be growing tired of leading the Christian life. It can be difficult to follow the moral laws of Christ and his Church, to participate every Sunday (without exception) at Mass with our families when we could easily be doing something else or simply staying in bed, and to challenge friends and family members to return to the Church in the face of admitted ridicule. The Christian life means to live in such a way that one's life would not make sense if God did not exist. To be a follower of Jesus demands no less nor more than what Jesus demanded of Peter.

There is a second aspect of this gospel passage worth considering. It is the reaction of Peter to the catch of fish. At the sight of that massive manifestation of divine power, that great number of fish, Peter made an incredible confession of faith: "Depart from me, Lord, for I am a sinful man." Peter came to terms with his sinfulness, his unworthiness to be an evangelizer for Christ. Not one of us is ever truly worthy to be an evangelizer. In the face of God's divine generosity, Peter was overwhelmed by his personal sinfulness and unworthiness. Something happened to him as it can to us when we follow the Word of God, when we encounter Christ in his all-powerful Word.

He must have experienced an interior liberation of sorts—or, as the penance manuals say, he was "convicted" of his sinfulness at that moment in the presence of the miracle of God. In effect, the power of Jesus revealed his sinfulness and, ultimately, the mercy of God.

Cardinal Carlo Martini perceptively summed up Peter's experience this way:

> At this point Peter finally grasps what the Gospel is in terms of salvation for sinful man, he grasps the true nature of God. For God is not someone who urges us to do better, not a moral reform-er of humanity but above all he is unlimited, boundless Love, offered freely and purely with a mercy which neither condemns nor accuses nor reproves. Jesus' look is not accusing or admoni-tory, it is simply a look of mercy and love: Peter, I love you even like this, I knew you were like this and I loved you knowing you were like this.
>
> In conclusion, we can say: Peter undergoes the *experience*, which is perhaps the easiest and the hardest in life, *of letting himself be loved.*[3]

So it is with us. So it must be with us if we are to be effective and credible evangelizers for the Lord. We must pray to come to terms with our own sinful-ness and repent often in confession. For the sacrament of Reconciliation is fundamental to all our efforts at evangelization. It is the citadel of divine mercy.

We must ask the Lord to take away from us everything that keeps us from him. Ultimately it is all God's favor, God's grace, his amazing grace, that brings us to him over and over again and strengthens us in our vocation to be his followers and evangelizers, sharing and witnessing to the Gospel each and every day.

The Lord continues to form us, too, as he did Peter. He continues to help us by the movement of the Holy Spirit within us. He continues to help us to follow his holy Word, to act on his holy Word, and even when facing disappointments in our apostolic efforts, to see "a great number of fish." He continues to bring us to our sinfulness and ultimately reassures us over and over again not to be afraid, for he loves us. That is what it means to be an evangelizer—to stand up for our precious faith in obvious and subtle ways. Peter learned that lesson on a boat with Jesus. He would learn it again and again. It is no less our daily experience, for Jesus is routinely in the boats of our lives. It will continue to be our experience if we stay close to his Word always, seek to understand and follow it, and encounter the living and merciful Lord in the process.

As men and women of the New Evangelization, we can see in this Lucan passage the life-changing power of God's holy Word. We are called to be fishers of men and women in our day, and we can be successful as Peter was. We are called, moreover, to repent of our sinfulness precisely in the moments of our apostolic success.

By being truly open to the Word of God, we are encouraged to go out into the deep. The fish are awaiting us—men and women open to the New Evangelization. They will receive him precisely because *we* listened and acted upon his holy Word. And most importantly, in these situations, we will encounter Jesus Christ ever anew and, like Peter, become changed men and women. Such is the unfailing power of the Word of God.

Reflect

1. Have you experienced an awe-inspiring encounter with God similar to Peter's? What was your response to it?

2. Is there anything in your life that Jesus is calling you to let go of in order to follow him more closely?

3. Jesus calls each of us, like Peter, to follow him in a particular way. How are you living out that call?

4. What is the "deep water" that you are being called to put out into?

Pray

Let us reflect and pray over these words of Blessed Pope John Paul II: "Do not be afraid to open the doors of your mind and heart to Christ and find honest truth and unconditional love."[4]

Let us listen to God's voice in Isaiah 41:
> Do not fear: I am with you;
> do not be anxious: I am your God.
> I will strengthen you, I will help you,
> I will uphold you with my victorious right hand. . . .
> For I am the LORD, your God,
> who grasp your right hand;
> It is I who say to you, Do not fear,
> I will help you. (Is 41:10, 13)

TWO

Preparing the Soil

What do we need to do (with the assistance, of course, of the Holy Spirit) that the Word of God might take hold in us and change and continue to transform us as it did St. Peter? What is our role as we seek to encounter Jesus today in his living Word, and what are the obstacles we will assuredly face?

In the first chapter, we see how a seemingly reluctant Peter "put out into the deep" at the Word of Jesus, at Jesus' command. Something miraculous ensued. In the face of an unexpected divine generosity on the part of our God, as manifested in the catch of an abundance of fish, Peter became a changed man, an evangelizer for the Lord. He encountered the living God in the following of his Word, and it changed him into a man of faith, a leader in the faith.

What about us? How open and ready are we to receive his living Word in our hearts and minds? In this second chapter we look at the parable of the sower (Mt 13:1–23) and reflect on preparing the soil for an encounter with the living Word of God. Benedict XVI alluded to this as he inaugurated the Year of Faith. He wrote:

The "door of faith" is always open for us, ush-
ering us into the life of communion with God
and offering entry into his Church. It is possible
to cross that threshold when the word of God
is proclaimed and the heart allows itself to be
shaped by transforming grace. (*PF* 1)

What is meant by the phrase "the heart allows itself
to be shaped by transforming grace"? Whenever the
Word of God is proclaimed, the transforming grace of
the Holy Spirit is active in this enterprise so that our
hearts might be shaped and transformed. The perennial challenge is to have our hearts and minds open
to this "shaping" and to understand what obstacles
prevent the shaping.

The parable of the sower speaks of the seed, the
Word of God, and the obstacles to that seed taking root:

On that day, Jesus went out of the house and sat
down by the sea. Such large crowds gathered
around him that he got into a boat and sat down,
and the whole crowd stood along the shore. And
he spoke to them at length in parables, saying:
"A sower went out to sow. And as he sowed,
some seed fell on the path, and birds came and
ate it up. Some fell on rocky ground, where it
had little soil. It sprang up at once because the
soil was not deep, and when the sun rose it was
scorched, and it withered for lack of roots. Some
seed fell among thorns, and the thorns grew up
and choked it. But some seed fell on rich soil, and
produced fruit, a hundred or sixty or thirtyfold.

> Whoever has ears ought to hear." The disciples
> approached him and said, "Why do you speak
> to them in parables?" He said to them in reply,
> "Because knowledge of the mysteries of the
> kingdom of heaven has been granted to you, but
> to them it has not been granted. To anyone who
> has, more will be given and he will grow rich;
> from anyone who has not, even what he has will
> be taken away." (Mt 13:1–12)

This text from St. Matthew is the only text in
sacred scripture of a parable *with* an explanation.
Upon closer study, this parable is not so much about
the sower but about the seeds and their yields—the
three unsuccessful plantings and the fourth one that
is superabundantly successful. It is about God's living Word, how he continues to speak to us, and what
some of the obstacles are to our hearing his Word.

The living Word is communicated to us in sacred
scripture *and* the living tradition of the Church. The
seed is his Word. We hear his Word as we ponder and
listen to sacred scripture, the writings of our Holy
Father, and every aspect of the living tradition of our
Church. At every Mass and in the various sacramental
encounters, for example, our God is speaking to us. Do
we ever stop to ponder what exactly we are hearing? In
fact, do we hear him? Do we recognize the sound of his
voice in the quiet of our hearts, in our perennial efforts
at prayer? What distractions get in our way? Are we
thinking about all that we need to do in our lives, or
are we able to hear his life-giving Word at this very
moment as we gather together today?

What can enslave us? What prevents us from hearing him? The gospel speaks of *three* specific types of soil that block our ability to hear his Word and keep us from him. For purposes of this parable, the seed is God's Word. And each of the four plantings speaks to us in different ways.

First, Jesus speaks of seed sown, or planted, on a path (i.e., uncultivated soil). The situation is akin to one who hears God's Word but fails to understand it. You and I have had that experience. We have often relied on misinformation as if it were the truth of our faith. In such situations, we are easy targets for "the evil one" who "comes and steals away what was sown" in our hearts. The evil one sees our lack of understanding or even misunderstanding with respect to God's Word as a real opportunity to undercut successfully a nascent faith.

How important, then, it is to study and read scripture each day and come to a deeper understanding of the teachings of our precious faith! The more we read prayerfully and study his Word, the more likely we will understand the depth and beauty of God's living voice. Moreover, "the Word of God is a principal tool in the formation of conscience when it is assimilated by study, prayer, and practice" (*USCCA* 314). That is another reason why Bible-study groups and teaching opportunities in the faith can be so helpful. Otherwise we remain enslaved by our ignorance. Speaking of scripture, St. Jerome writes, "Ignorance of scripture is ignorance of Christ." That is also true with respect to the teachings of our faith.

To this end Benedict XVI inaugurated the Year of Faith. He wrote concretely:

> Evidently, knowledge of the content of faith is essential for giving one's own *assent,* that is to say for adhering fully with intellect and will to what the Church proposes. Knowledge of faith opens a door into the fullness of the saving mystery revealed by God. . . . In order to arrive at a systematic knowledge of the content of the faith, all can find in the *Catechism of the Catholic Church* a precious and indispensable tool. It is one of the most important fruits of the *Second Vatican Council.* . . . It is in this sense that the Year of Faith will have to see a concerted effort to rediscover and study the fundamental content of the faith that receives its systematic and organic synthesis in the *Catechism of the Catholic Church.* . . . The *Catechism* provides a permanent record of the many ways in which the Church has meditated on the faith and made progress in doctrine so as to offer certitude to believers in their lives of faith. . . . On page after page, we find that what is presented here is no theory, but an encounter with a Person who lives within the Church. (*PF* 10–11; emphasis added)

Understanding the faith is thus key lest the soil remain an uncultivated "path."

Second, Jesus speaks of seed sown, on rocky ground. This is akin to hearing God's word initially with joy, but the joy lasts only a brief period because there are no roots. It is a superficial faith, a personal shallowness. Our lives can easily be filled with new projects, which seem initially exciting but then are abandoned when the going gets rough or when the demands of time to acquire and perfect a new skill seem too much. There is not enough time, or more accurately stated, we fail to give the appropriate time to developing a hobby, a sport, or a language. Similarly, it can happen with his Word: we do not give it the time it requires.

We need to set aside appropriate time with the Word of God so that the roots might become a part of us. Otherwise we become prone to some tribulation or persecution, and the joy of encountering the Lord Jesus in his Word lasts for a brief time.

And encountering God's Word is best done in silence, an increasing novelty in a world defined by social networking and the addictive behavior that it seems to produce. In a prophetic way, Benedict XVI spoke to this modern-day challenge and phenomenon:

> Technical progress, especially in the area of transport and communications, has made human life more comfortable but also more keyed up, at times even frantic. Cities are almost always noisy, silence is rarely to be found in them because there is always background noise, in some areas even at night. . . .

The youngest, who were already born into this condition, seem to want to fill every empty moment with music and images, as for fear of feeling this very emptiness. This is a trend that has always existed, especially among the young and in the more developed urban contexts but today it has reached a level such as to give rise to talk about anthropological mutation. Some people are no longer capable of remaining for long periods in silence and solitude. . . .

I shall sum it up like this: by withdrawing into silence and solitude, human beings, so to speak, "expose" themselves to reality in their nakedness, to that apparent "void," which I mentioned at the outset, in order to experience instead Fullness, the presence of God, of the most royal Reality that exists and that lies beyond the tangible dimension.[5]

It is thus in silence that his Word can take root. For sure, life is a rocky road for each and every one of us. We can be enslaved by our inability to see how it is that God's Word has within it a courage and grace to help us joyfully bear witness to the Word in our homes and workplaces—a courage that sets us free. It is with this courage and grace that we can resist the tribulations and persecutions that come our way and draw energy from an enrooted and life-giving Word of God.

Third, Jesus speaks of seed sown, among thorns— one who hears God's Word, but then worldly anxiety and the lure of riches choke it off. There are competitive forces at work here. In a subtle, or perhaps not-so-subtle way, they compete for our time with God and his holy Word. You and I experience this each and every day of our lives. We so often struggle with this challenge and worry about it, for we know that we need God and that God desires to be our friend.

But how often do we hear the refrain that there are not enough hours in the day? I feel that pressure each and every day. It can cause anxiety. You know this reality very well: a world challenged by billable hours, patients and clients, countless meetings, income, clout, connections, powerful positions, the demands of instant communications, prestigious offices and titles, and maybe even work itself. These are all causes for our anxiety, and they make it difficult and (if we are not careful) even impossible to hear the Word of God on a regular basis. His Word becomes choked.

We cannot finish this section on the choking off of the Word of God without a special word of encouragement to parents. You have the great and wonderful challenge of raising children today with so many sports and activities that consume your limited time. You parents are challenged at every turn. God bless you for your constant care of our children! At the same time, your particular fears and anxieties can enslave you if you are not careful and attentive. And there will be no way for his holy Word to withstand the thorns that choke it.

It is important to name the anxieties in our lives. What are they? It might take some time to come to terms with those things that burden us and make us anxious. How do they preoccupy us and keep us away from appropriating his living Word?

Not only does this gospel text speak about anxiety as a cause for our not hearing the Word of God, but it also refers to the lure of riches. Yes, it is the temptation to look over the fence at the riches or seeming happiness of others. In so doing, we simply refuse to hear his Word because we are preoccupied inordinately with the riches of others. That can distract us from the priorities that should feed us, the life-giving and freeing priorities that Jesus reveals in the living Word of God.

Do we inordinately desire riches? Are we so oriented in that direction that our life is defined by this desire? If so, we need to confront that inordinate desire. For it keeps us away from God's holy Word. Scripture tells us that it can choke the Word and prevent us from bearing fruit.

Benedict XVI spoke about a deeper level as well: "Quite frequently both in the Old and in the New Testament, we find sin described as a *refusal to hear the word*, as a *breaking of the covenant* and thus as being closed to God who calls us to communion with himself" (*VD* 26). In effect, the refusal to hear his Word is the root of sin. But it need not remain at that level. When we accept the forgiveness of Jesus, the Word of God opens us up to salvation.

Finally, and in rather contrasting and more hopeful language, we hear of "the seed sown on rich soil [and] . . . the one who hears the word and understands it, who indeed bears fruit and yields a hundred, or sixty or thirtyfold." This seed is the person who hears and understands and studies and lives God's Word. God's Word does not fall on a path, or rocky soil, or thorns. No, his Word bears fruit and yields a hundred or sixty or thirty fold. That is our hope and our goal in life.

During an address at the Vatican to Church leaders involved in the New Evangelization, Benedict XVI outlined a hopeful vision of evangelization, saying, "The word of God continues to grow and to spread." One reason he gave was "that the seed of the word, as the Gospel Parable of the Sower recounts, still falls on good soil that welcomes it and produces fruit. . . . In the world, even if evil makes more noise, good soil continues to exist."[6]

The great twentieth-century Scottish Protestant preacher and theologian William Barclay describes the good soil as similar to the person whose "mind is open":

> He is at all times willing to learn. He is prepared to hear. He is never either too proud or too busy to listen. Many a man would have been saved all kinds of heartbreak, if he had simply stopped to listen to the voice of a wise friend, or to the voice of God. He understands. He has thought the thing out and knows what this means for him, and is prepared to accept it. He translates his hearing into action. He produces the good fruit of the good seed. The real hearer is the man who listens, who understands, and who obeys.[7]

It is then that we have the freedom of God's children, set free from all that enslaves us. God's holy Word will change us, transform our hearts into him, if only the soil is prepared to receive his Word. That is our perennial challenge if we are to encounter the Lord God in his holy Word. Like snow and rain, this encounter with God's Word impregnates not only the earth but also each of us who believes; and it impregnates us with his precious life. Stated differently, in the words of St. Paul to the early Christians at Thessalonica: "For this reason we too give thanks to God unceasingly, that, in receiving the word of God from hearing us, you received not a human word but, as it truly is, the word of God, which is now at work in you who believe" (1 Thes 2:13). And, in the words of the gospel, we rejoice because: "the seed that falls on good ground will yield a fruitful harvest."[8] Yes, it is a seed at work in us, a seed that cries out to be shared and will be shared in the power of his Holy Spirit. Happy planting!

Reflect

Read again the parable of the sower (Matthew 13:1–12).

1. Why do you fail to understand God's Word? Is it through inattention, lack of effort, or failure to take the time?

2. In what ways is your soul like rocky ground? Is it because of personal shallowness, distractions, busyness, preoccupations, or some other reason?

3. In what ways do the thorns choke off your

reception of the Word? Is it because of your
anxieties and fears? Is it because of your
ambitions and desires? Is it in another way?

4. What is the place of silence in your prayer and
    reflection on the Word?

Pray

Prayer for the New Evangelization

Heavenly Father,
pour forth your Holy Spirit to inspire me with these
    words from holy scripture.
Stir in my soul the desire to renew my faith and
    deepen my relationship with your Son, our
    Lord Jesus Christ, so that I might truly believe
    in and live the Good News.
Open my heart to hear the Gospel, and grant
    me the confidence to proclaim the Good News
    to others.
Pour out your Spirit, so that I might be
    strengthened to go forth and witness to
    the Gospel in my everyday life through my
    words and actions.
In moments of hesitation, remind me:
If not me, then who will proclaim the Gospel?
If not now, then when will the Gospel
    be proclaimed?
If not the truth of the Gospel, then what shall
    I proclaim?

God, our Father, I pray that through the Holy Spirit
I might hear the call of the New Evangelization
to deepen my faith, grow in confidence to
proclaim the Gospel, and boldly witness to the
saving grace of your Son, Jesus Christ, who
lives and reigns with you, in the unity of the
Holy Spirit, one God, for ever and ever.
Amen.[9]

THREE

The Word Became Flesh and Made His Dwelling among Us

When we speak of "the Word [who] became flesh and made his dwelling among us" (Jn 1:14), we are speaking of the incarnate Jesus, the Jesus who was born at Christmas and dwells among us still. "The Greek term for flesh, *sarx*, is very close to the Hebrew *basar*; it denotes man as a fragile, transitory, mortal being. The Word who was 'with God' and 'was God' (see Jn 1:1) thus becomes true man—a visible, palpable, mortal being dwelling in space and time."[10] He is also truly God.

We can never forget that "the Incarnation is the unsurpassable height and the absolute fulfillment of salvation history. Jesus Christ is God's final and definitive word to humankind (Heb 1:2), the sole mediator between God and men (1 Tim 2:5; see Heb 8:6; 9:15; 12:24), the source of all salvation, both now and in the future (see Acts 4:12)."[11]

Only the incarnate Word can teach us the knowledge of God. It is as if a veil had hidden God from us. In his first letter, St. John refers to Jesus as the Word of "life." He says, speaking of the Word of life, "For the life was made visible . . . that was with the

Father and was made visible to us" (1 Jn 1:2). It is the same Jesus who had been prophesized in the Hebrew scriptures. We hear from the letter to the Hebrews: "In times past, God spoke in partial and various ways to our ancestors through the prophets; in these last days, he spoke to us through a son" (Heb 1:2). And that Son is the Word of God. The prophet Isaiah tells us, for example, that a "shoot shall spring from the stump of Jesse" (Is 11:1) and that "a child is born to us. [And] they name him Wonder-Counselor, God-Hero, Father-Forever, Prince of Peace" (Is 9:5). As the Word became flesh, the invisibility of our God is thus interrupted. You and I know in retrospect that Isaiah is speaking of Jesus, "the image of the invisible God" (Col 1:15).

There are many witnesses who have encountered Jesus. In this chapter we focus on the *infant* Jesus and seek to encounter him anew with those witnesses. At his birth, there were five such witnesses: the angels; the shepherds; the magi; Joseph; and, of course, Mary, his mother. We cannot help but remember the many details of that holy night when Jesus was born that have been revealed to us in the Word of God. As we look at these five witnesses, I invite you to encounter Jesus in his living Word, for he is the Word of God.

The angels: The angels announced to the shepherds "the good news of great joy" about the birth of Christ. We hear that "suddenly there was a multitude of the heavenly host with the angel, praising God and saying, 'Glory to God in the highest and on earth peace to those on whom his favor rests'" (Lk 2:13–14).

Instinctively, in the face of the infant Jesus, the angels were moved to pray and sing his praises. They sang the same hymn that we sing at Mass more than two thousand years later—that hymn of praise and peace of that holy night, the Gloria. As we contemplate the Word of God in the infant Jesus with the angels of that night, are we not moved to prayer, to hymns of praise? According to Blessed John Paul II in *Evangelium Vitae (The Gospel of Life)*, "the source of this 'great joy' (sung by the angel) is the Birth of the Savior; but Christmas also reveals the full meaning of every human birth, and the joy which accompanies the birth of the Messiah is thus seen to be the foundation and fulfillment of joy at every child born into the world" (*EV* 1). It is thus good for each of us to ponder the birth of Jesus; and with the hymn that accompanied that great mystery, we are called to sing and praise the birth of every child. So precious are children in the eyes of our Savior, who was one like them.

The shepherds: "When the angels went away from them to heaven, the shepherds said to one another, 'Let us go, then, to Bethlehem to see this thing that has taken place, which the Lord has made known to us'" (Lk 2:15). And so they went in haste and they were amazed at what they saw. The poor have always been drawn to Jesus, almost instinctively. Even in his infancy, born humbly in the wood of a manger, Jesus was someone with whom the poor could identify and to whom they were drawn like a magnet. There is a poverty in each one of us. It is in this condition that we continue to encounter the Word of God. He speaks to us in our poverty.

Describing Jesus' birth, St. Ignatius of Loyola in his *Spiritual Exercises* writes, "Not only does He hide His divinity under the guise of humanity, but He debases His humanity itself to the infirmities and weaknesses of infancy."[12] Describing Jesus' poverty, a poverty which had to have attracted the shepherds, he writes further, "He is born in a strange country, out of His mother's house, where He would have found what is never wanting even to the most neglected of poor children, a roof to shelter Him and a cradle to rest in."[13] The cave is open to wind and rain. It can be said of him with credibility that "foxes have dens and birds of the sky have nests; but the Son of man has nowhere to rest his head" (Lk 9:58).

With the poor shepherds, we too contemplate the infant Jesus. We remember anew his Word in the first beatitude, "Blessed are the poor in spirit, for theirs is the kingdom of heaven" (Mt 5:3). The poverty marking the face of the Word made flesh was his choice. In the words of St. Ignatius of Loyola, "He quitted heaven and His glory. Above all, understand the necessity of detachment, and be persuaded that disengagement from creatures is the only true way which leads to God."[14] The infant Jesus reveals to us this detachment, as did the shepherds who came to visit him.

The magi: Seeing a star, the magi from the East came to pay the child homage. In fact, scripture tells us, "They were overjoyed at seeing the star, and on entering the house they saw the child with Mary his mother. They prostrated themselves and did him homage" (Mt 2:10–11). Opening their treasure, they offered him gifts of gold, frankincense, and myrrh. The star was replaced by an infant face—a face, a Word, which provoked in them a generosity with gifts and deep gratitude. The magi story is one of discovery and a journey of faith. They were led to the infant Jesus. In his infancy, do we, as they, not see our faith in a nurturing phase? Their gifts are a response to *the* gift, a response to him, and a grateful expression of the inestimable gift of their discovered faith; for at its base, Epiphany is truly an exchange of gifts.

You and I exchange gifts each time we offer ourselves at holy Mass. Our gifts are represented by the bread and wine that are transformed into his body and blood—truly a wonderful exchange of gifts. Do we not see the face of Jesus in the host, the face of Jesus as infant, as risen, as truly the Son of God and Son of Mary? Do we not hear the Word of God every time it is spoken at Mass in the power of the Holy Spirit, the same Word who took on flesh and dwells among us?

Joseph: Throughout the entire drama of this holy night and those holy days, Joseph, the foster father, the guardian of the Redeemer, stands as the fourth eyewitness—as a devoted, faithful, and faith-filled witness—not seeming to comprehend fully what was happening. In so many pictures of the infant Jesus, we see Joseph. So often, in contrast to Joseph we are mere bystanders to the mystery of faith, not always full of faith. We see Jesus' face, but somehow we are not quite sure of its meaning. In time, the fullness of the mystery is revealed to us. The Word became flesh and dwelt among us. Like Joseph, we remain faithful and ever ready to guard the gift of faith, the person of Jesus, given to us out of love, particularly as our faith develops.

Mary: Finally, the fifth witness is Mary, our Blessed Mother. In fact, she is the preeminent witness that night and throughout the life of her Son. Through her lens, we learn much about her and about Jesus.

Speaking of the preeminence of Mary, Blessed John Paul II wrote in his beautiful encyclical letter *Redemptoris Mater* (*Mother of the Redeemer*), "For the Church of that time and of every time Mary is a *singular* witness to the years of Jesus' infancy and hidden life at Nazareth, when she 'kept all these things, pondering them in her heart'" (*RM* 26; emphasis added).

And there is a special relationship between the infant Jesus, the Word made flesh, and his mother, Mary. That is true about every mother and child. The care, love, and nurturing between a mother and child underscore the vital importance of that relationship.

One of my personal habits on Thanksgiving Day each year is to look again at my Christmas cards from the previous year before discarding them. When I did just that again this past year, I was surprised and actually delighted with the number of cards that featured the infant Jesus and his mother, Mary. The artists portrayed this relationship in so many different ways. Each portrayal speaks so much about the artist and can also feed us in our spiritual contemplation.

Here is what I found in the various cards—the child Jesus being held by Mary and touching the head, almost blessing the head, of one of the magi; the child Jesus sleeping in the lap of his mother as she looks at him; the child resting on the ground with the Blessed Virgin kneeling before him; the child lying in the manger reaching up to grab a lamb with Mary kneeling before him; the child, with his feet on a pillow, reaching for Mary's neck; Jesus reaching for grapes while being held by Mary; Mary holding the child close to her as he touches her neck; Mary holding the child so all can see him smiling; Jesus being held by Mary with his eyes closed; Mary holding the white blanket open so that all can see Jesus; Jesus looking at Mary while holding her face and breast; Mary holding the child with angels surrounding him; Mary holding the child up high with Jesus giving a wooden cross to the baby John the Baptist; Mary holding the child close to her, contemplating his face; Jesus being held by his mother as he holds her chin; Mary holding Jesus as he pulls a flower from a pot; Mary crossing her hands on her chest as Jesus lies on her lap.

In all of these various artistic representations, it is clear that what they have in common is that the *infant* Jesus is the object of the love of his mother and all those around him: Jesus, the Word of God, the Son of God and Son of Mary.

How can one separate the love of a son, this Son, from the love of his mother?

> The one who accepted "Life" in the name of all and for the sake of all was Mary, the Virgin Mother; she is thus most closely and personally associated with the Gospel of life. . . . Through her acceptance and loving care for the life of the Incarnate Word, human life has been rescued from condemnation to final and eternal death. (*EV* 102)

And the gospel of life takes on new meaning.

For a deeper understanding of the role of our Blessed Lady in the birth of her Son, I wish to consider briefly what it means that the Son of God was "incarnate of the Virgin Mary"—a five word change in the translation of the Creed for the liturgy. Father Anthony Lickteig, of the Archdiocese of Washington, wrote beautifully of this change for our parish bulletin for the First Sunday of Advent. He wrote:

> The Word of God took his flesh, his humanity, from Mary. Mary's pregnancy was not of a surrogate nature; she truly is the mother of the Son of God in every way. This is what we mean when we will say that the Son of God "was incarnate of the Virgin Mary."[15]

It is worth pondering—this incredible mystery and teaching of our faith.

Now a fundamental question: what does the infant Jesus, the incarnate Word, say to us today and for all ages? The infant Jesus, born at Bethlehem, speaks to us as he did to them in his day.

> This saving event reveals to humanity not only
> the boundless love of God who "so loved the
> world that he gave his only Son" (Jn 3:16), but
> also the incomparable value of every human per-
> son. (*EV* 2)

He has united himself to each and every human being precisely by his Incarnation.

That is precisely why the Church continu- ally stands publicly for the protection of life, every human life, from conception through natural death. Life is linked, in special fashion, to the birth of Christ himself. At its deepest level, then, in the words of St. Athanasius of old, "The Son of God became man so that we might become God" (i.e., to share forever in his divine destiny).

As we contemplate—with Mary—her Son, the infant Jesus, can we not see in him the face of every child? Does the Word of God, whom we encounter in the infant, not speak to each and every one of us in a unique and very personal way?

When we speak of encountering the Word of God in our day, more than two millennia later, we are thus challenged to place ourselves with our five wit- nesses—Our Lady and Joseph and the angels, shep- herds, and magi. With the aid of the Holy Spirit, we are challenged anew to ponder—as Mary did—the Word of God who is Son of God and Son of Mary as a helpless little child.

Each of us still comes in our poverty to him, is led by a star, is moved to prayer in song, sees in him a fig- ure of every child born and unborn, remains a devoted witness and faithful bystander, and is inspired to give gifts to others because of him. Each of us hears his Word and encounters God in his Word, a Word made flesh and dwelt among us out of love.

Each contemplates the infant Jesus in a different but sure way and hears his Word as his Word is given to us. In the infant Jesus, the Word became flesh and dwelt among us. The drama of that specific holy night—and it was not a one-night stand—continues at every moment in history and will never end until we see him face-to-face and hear his Word for all eternity.

Reflect

Read again about the birth of Jesus (Luke 2:1–20 and Matthew 2:1–12).

1. Where is the poverty in your life that is a place of encounter with the Word of God?

2. What does "poverty of spirit" mean for you?

3. What do the gifts of bread and wine that we present at Mass symbolize in your life?

4. How would you answer the question: What does the infant Jesus, the incarnate Word, say to us today?

Pray

Pray this section of the Nicene Creed slowly and reflectively:

> I believe in one Lord Jesus Christ,
> the Only Begotten Son of God,
> born of the Father before all ages.
> God from God, Light from Light,
> true God from true God,
> begotten, not made, consubstantial with the Father;
> through him all things were made.
> For us men and for our salvation
> he came down from heaven,
> and by the Holy Spirit was incarnate of the
>   Virgin Mary,
> and became man.
> For our sake he was crucified under Pontius Pilate,
> he suffered death and was buried,
> and rose again on the third day
> in accordance with the Scriptures.
> He ascended into heaven
> and is seated at the right hand of the Father.
> He will come again in glory
> to judge the living and the dead
> and his kingdom will have no end.

Part II:
Encountering Jesus
in the Sacraments

FOUR

Baptism as Gateway

We have reflected in the first three chapters on our encounter with Jesus in his Word. The next three chapters focus on our encounter with him in the sacraments. And then finally we look at the encounter with Jesus in the service of charity. We begin with Baptism, the gateway to the Christian life.

In Baptism we become members of the Body of Christ, the Church, and we encounter Jesus in the waters of Baptism. Our Baptism is, after all, intimately linked to and given meaning through the Baptism of our Lord Jesus Christ. We read in Mark's account of the Baptism of Jesus by John:

> And this is what [John] proclaimed: "One mightier than I is coming after me. I am not worthy to stoop and loosen the thongs of his sandals. I have baptized you with water; he will baptize you with the holy Spirit." It happened in those days that Jesus came from Nazareth of Galilee and was baptized in the Jordan by John. On coming up out of the water he saw the heavens being torn open and the Spirit, like a dove, descending upon him. And a voice came from the heavens,

"You are my beloved Son; with you I am well
pleased." (Mk 1:7–11)

The gospel image of Jesus, in each of the three
texts describing his Baptism, is a most striking one.
Imagine Jesus coming out of the water after being
baptized by his cousin John the Baptist. He sees the
heavens open and the Spirit descending on him like
a dove. And, yes, akin to another Epiphany, he hears
the voice of his Father booming out from heaven and
naming him: "You are my beloved Son; with you I am
well pleased." The Father identifies for all times Jesus
as his Son, the Son of God. What a profound picture
of the Trinity—the Father, Son, and Holy Spirit—three
persons in one God.

The feast of the Baptism of the Lord, celebrated in
January, is the last of the Christmas feasts. You might
wonder about its connection to Christmas. St. Maximus
of Turin writes:

> At Christmas he was born a man; today he is
> reborn sacramentally. . . . That is why the Lord
> Jesus went to the river for baptism (albeit many
> years after his birth), he wanted his holy body to
> be washed in the Jordan's water.[16]

Benedict XVI stood on the shores of that same Jordan
River during his pilgrimage to the Holy Land and
proclaimed, "Jesus stood in line with sinners and ac-
cepted John's baptism of penance as a prophetic sign
of his own passion, death and resurrection for the
forgiveness of sins."[17] By that most memorable and
humble action of our God, Jesus makes the waters of

Baptism holy and ready for you and me. Jesus gives us an unforgettable example. Moreover, at the Jordan, he identifies dramatically with those of us he came to save—sinners such as you and me.

As if to underscore and explain the importance of Baptism, Benedict XVI's first chapter in his book *Jesus of Nazareth: From the Baptism in the Jordan to the Transfiguration*, is titled "The Baptism of Jesus." He emphasizes that Jesus *inaugurates* his public ministry in the waters of the Jordan by his Baptism by John the Baptist. Benedict XVI writes:

> Jesus' Baptism anticipated his death on the cross, and the heavenly voice proclaimed an antici-pation of the Resurrection. These anticipations have now become reality. John's Baptism with water has received its full meaning through the Baptism of Jesus' own life and death. . . .
>
> To accept the invitation to be baptized now means to go to the place of Jesus' Baptism. It is to go where he identifies himself with us and to receive our identification with him. The point where he anticipates death has now become the point where we anticipate rising again with him.[18]

Baptism is the place where we encounter Jesus. The Baptism of Jesus was so important for him that his final words in Matthew's gospel, his mission state-ment to his disciples, were, "Go therefore and make disciples of all nations, baptizing them in the name of the Father, and of the Son, and of the holy Spirit" (Mt

28:19). It was not a suggestion. It was a commission, a mission, and a command, which has been followed from that very pronouncement of Jesus to our day. Referring to these words, Benedict XVI writes:

> The Baptism that Jesus' disciples have been administering since he spoke those words is an entrance into the master's own Baptism—into the reality that he anticipated by means of it. That is the way to become a Christian."[19]

Baptism is thus the gateway to the Christian life, the gateway sacrament. It is our dying and rising with Jesus. We encounter him there.

At one point in our lives, the day of our Baptism, you and I have gone to the place of Jesus' Baptism. On that day, we became children of his Father, members of his living body, the Church, and temples of the Holy Spirit. How privileged we were and continue to be. Baptized into him, we received the same Holy Spirit that he received as a man; and the Spirit's manifold gifts are given to us as well. Pope St. Leo the Great explains:

> Through the sacrament of Baptism, you have become a temple of the Holy Spirit. Do not drive away so great a guest by evil conduct and become again a slave to the devil, for your liberty was bought by the blood of the Christ.[20]

Typically, we do not celebrate our baptismal day. And yet, for Christians, the day of our Baptism is the most important day of our lives. It is the day we enter the Church. (Baptism is the first of the three sacraments of initiation.) It is the day when we are *plunged* (and that is what Baptism means in Greek) into the very life of God. "Yet I live, no longer I who live, but Christ lives in me" (Gal 2:20). The baptized have "put on Christ" (Gal 3:27). Baptism is birth into the new life of Christ. It is the beginning of our walk with Jesus.

If we had listened carefully (or our godparents had listened for us), we could undoubtedly, have heard those same words of the Father naming us his sons and daughters in Christ Jesus. These are powerful words at the beginning of the baptismal rite when the priest or deacon says: "I claim you for Christ our savior by the sign of his cross."

Another point of the rite worth emphasizing is the Profession of Faith. It is, in effect, a question-and-answer version of the Apostles' Creed, which was used in Rome by candidates for Baptism. In a homily given at Regensburg, Germany, on September 12, 2006, Benedict XVI points out:

> The Creed is not a collection of propositions; it is not a theory. It is anchored in the event of Baptism—a genuine encounter between God and man. In the mystery of Baptism, God stoops to meet us; he comes close to us and in turn brings us closer to one another. Baptism means that Jesus Christ adopts us as his brothers and sisters, welcoming us as sons and daughters into God's family.

Perhaps it is wise that we do not celebrate our baptismal *day*, for that might just emphasize too much "the event" of our Baptism. As important as that day is, it is only the beginning of our initiation into the very life, death, and resurrection of Jesus. As St. Paul teaches us:

> Are you unaware that we who were baptized into Christ Jesus were baptized into his death? We were indeed buried with him through baptism into death, so that, just as Christ was raised from the dead by the glory of the Father, we too might live in newness of life. (Rom 6:3–4)

Thus, for us, as baptized Christians, our Baptism triggers a lifetime venture, a lifetime challenge. It is a day that initiated us into a daily encounter with Christ, who has claimed us. We have a lifelong vocation of dying and rising with Christ in the power of the Holy Spirit, of sharing in the very concrete mission of Jesus in our specific daily lives.

But what does it mean to share in the mission of Jesus, a mission born at Baptism, a mission of encounter? The anointing at Baptism with sacred chrism signifies that the newly baptized person is incorporated into Christ himself, who was "anointed" priest, prophet, and king. As baptized Christians, we have the privilege of sharing first-hand in the priestly, prophetic, and kingly mission of Jesus himself—lives of service and love for others. In our day, a renewed sense of missionary zeal and fervor is required! This is, after all, the time of the New Evangelization. As Cardinal Donald Wuerl said at Rome on October 8, 2012, at the Synod on the New Evangelization for the Transmission of the Christian Faith: "The New Evangelization must rest upon the theological understanding that it is Christ who reveals man to himself, man's true identity in Christ, the new Adam."[21] And this dimension of the New Evangelization has very practical implications for each of us.

What is our share today in the "priestly" mission of Jesus? The priestly mission is not reserved only for those of us who are members of the clergy. To share in his priestly mission means sharing in the sacrificial offering of Jesus, which reached its fulfillment on the Cross—all out of love for us. Each time we sacrifice out of love for someone else, we share in the priestly mission of Jesus in our day. The operative word is "sacrifice." And it began on the day of our Baptism. In effect, each time we are agents of self-gift to another, we share in the priestly mission, and we encounter Jesus in the process.

The ordained priest shares uniquely in the priestly mission of Jesus when he offers the "sacrifice" of the Mass. There we have that holy exchange of gifts, that sacrificial offering, which is a reenactment of the dying and rising of Jesus carried out once and for all for our salvation.

The Second Vatican Council taught, with respect to the priestly mission of the laity:

> For all their works, prayers and apostolic en-
> deavors, their ordinary married and family life,

their daily occupations, their physical and mental relaxation, if carried out in the Spirit, and
even the hardships of life, if patiently borne—all
these become "spiritual sacrifices acceptable to
God through Jesus Christ." (1 Pt 2:5; *LG* 34)

What about our share in the "prophetic" mission
of Jesus? For sure it does not mean being a seer with
a crystal ball foretelling the future. Biblically under-
stood, a prophet is one who falls in love with God's
holy Word. And Baptism gives us the grace and ability and responsibility of accepting the Word of God.
We are called to proclaim it fearlessly, humbly, and
concretely in word and deed. This means falling in
love with God's Word, the Word made flesh, with
Jesus himself in whom we have been incorporated by
Baptism.

We should resolve to make the Word of God a
more regular part of our prayer lives. One concrete
way we can live the prophetic mission of Jesus in our
lives is to prepare for the Sunday readings throughout
the week. Gradually, with the help of the Holy Spirit,
our perspective on life begins to change; and we look
at the world and act in the world in the context of his
prophetic mission, which we share by virtue of our
Baptism. Little by little, we see the world through the
lens of God's holy Word and make our choices and
perform our actions on the basis of his holy Word.

In contrast to the clear share of the laity in the prophetic mission of Jesus, the ordained priest shares in
the prophetic mission of Jesus by his preaching and
teaching. It is perhaps the most challenging part of a

priest's share in the prophetic mission of Jesus in our contemporary world—a world adopting more and more a culture of death instead of a culture of life, a world where secularism and materialism and individualism so often prevail. And yet it is uniquely a part of the work of the priest to give prophetic witness of the Good News from the pulpit and from his life.

Finally, what about the "kingly" (or "royal") mission? Through Baptism, each of us shares in this mission of Jesus as well. In living out this mission, we encounter him each and every day. It requires of us to be a servant king, which is truly a countercultural sign in a world becoming more and more secular. It is to challenge our world each and every day in our workplaces and at home in ways of peace, justice, and joy in the power of the Holy Spirit.

St. Paul, after all, says that the kingdom of God exists where there is "righteousness, peace, and joy in the holy Spirit" (Rom 14:17). The challenge for each of us—our share in Jesus' royal mission—is to move the world in its quest for righteousness and peace; live and model the beatitudes; and, most concretely, follow the commandments to love God and neighbor. This royal mission takes place not primarily on the altars of our churches but in the workplaces and in our homes. And it is in the family that we are first trained in the mission of righteousness and peace; the family is the first school of righteousness and peace. It is there where we learn to share in Jesus' kingly mission concretely—a mission born on the day of our Baptism.

In his World Day of Peace message for 2012, Benedict XVI spoke providentially of justice:

> In this world of ours, in which, despite the profession of good intentions, the value of the person, of human dignity and human rights is seriously threatened by the widespread tendency to have recourse exclusively to the criteria of utility, profit and material possessions, it is important not to detach the concept of justice from its transcendent roots. Justice, indeed, is not simply a human convention, since what is just is ultimately determined not by positive law, but by the profound identity of the human being. It is the integral vision of man that saves us from falling into a contractual conception of justice and enables us to locate justice within the horizon of solidarity and love. (January 1, 2012)

In addition to the lay faithful, the ordained priest shares uniquely in the kingly mission of Jesus when he reconciles people to God, to neighbor, to the Church, and to each other through the sacrament of Penance, which has been referred to as the sacrament of the New Evangelization. And how important that is, in our increasingly broken world, a world which seems to feast on division, strife, and war! The priest is a man of peace. He is one whose ministry it is to heal and unify a people, a parish, and a community in the name of Jesus. His role is to guide with a gentle arm and a shepherd's heart all those to whom he is sent in the power of the Holy Spirit—especially the ill, poor, and most vulnerable. It is with these people that the priest shares in the kingly mission of Jesus and encounters Jesus.

Remember the day of your Baptism! The anointing at Baptism is our share in Christ's life and mission and our encounter with him. Baptism is also the source of our vocation, our call to holiness. This vocation stems from our Baptism, and it is lived out in different ways.

For some, it is the call or vocation to the married life, a life in Christ as husbands and wives possibly with the joy and responsibility of children. For others, it is the single life, a life called to live the challenge of our Baptism, the challenge of sacrificial love as a single man or woman in the workplace, our friendships, and all that we do.

And still for others, it is the call to priesthood, the diaconate, or the consecrated life—a wonderful life of total consecration to God. I thank God each day for the challenging yet wonderful ministry and life of my priesthood and for the people I have been sent to serve in so many ways.

Whatever our individual vocation, we can never forget our Baptism. We celebrate and give thanks, moreover, for our own Baptism, the basis of our shared vocations to holiness lived out in so many different ways. Baptism is the gateway to the Christian life.

Could there be any more profound and beautiful gift than the gift of Baptism? I speak of a gift that makes us like Christ, a gift that makes it possible for us to live with him now and forevermore. It is a gift that moves us to a daily exercise of Christian love. And it all came about because of what happened and was prefigured at the Jordan River many centuries ago. And the waters continue to pour from that same river made holy by the Baptism of Jesus, our Savior. It is a sacramental encounter with him who made the waters of that river holy forever.

Reflect

Read again about the Baptism of Jesus (Mark 1:7–11).

1. Allow the words of the Father to Jesus to resonate in your own heart: "You are my beloved son; you are my beloved daughter." How do these words affect you?

2. How do you share in the priestly mission of Christ?

3. How do you share in the prophetic mission of Christ?

4. How do you share in the kingly mission of Christ?

Pray

Let us pray that we will be faithful to our Baptism.

> Almighty, eternal God,
> when the Spirit descended upon Jesus
> at his baptism in the Jordan,
> you revealed him as your own beloved Son.
> Keep us, your children, born of water
>   and the Spirit,
> faithful to our calling.
> We ask this through our Lord Jesus Christ,
>   your Son,
> who lives and reigns with you and the Holy Spirit,
> one God for ever and ever. Amen.[22]

FIVE

Healing of the Paralytic:
A Paradigm for Forgiveness

A second way that we encounter Jesus through the sacraments is in the sacrament of Penance. The gospel story of Jesus healing a paralytic man offers us many rich lessons and is a wonderful paradigm of forgiveness. Our text is taken from Mark's gospel.

> When Jesus returned to Capernaum after some days, it became known that he was at home. Many gathered together so that there was no longer room for them, not even around the door, and he preached the word to them. They came bringing to him a paralytic carried by four men. Unable to get near Jesus because of the crowd, they opened up the roof above him. After they had broken through, they let down the mat on which the paralytic was lying. When Jesus saw their faith, he said to the paralytic, "Child, your sins are forgiven." Now some of the scribes were sitting there asking themselves, "Why does this man speak that way? He is blaspheming. Who but God alone can forgive sins?" Jesus immediately knew in his mind what they were thinking

to themselves, so he said, "Why are you thinking such things in your hearts? Which is easier, to say to the paralytic, 'Your sins are forgiven,' or to say, 'Rise, pick up your mat and walk'? But that you may know that the Son of Man has authority to forgive sins on earth"—he said to the paralytic, "I say to you, rise, pick up your mat, and go home." He rose, picked up his mat at once, and went away in the sight of everyone. They were all astounded and glorified God, saying, "We have never seen anything like this." (Mk 2:1–12)

There could not be a more dramatic gospel text, a perfect gospel upon which to meditate about forgiveness. The text incorporates three fundamental themes that are so essential to the work of each of us who seek to follow Jesus more closely and understand the heart of his mission—to encounter Jesus himself. The themes are evangelization, reconciliation, and celebration.

We first look more closely at the actual gospel text. In fact, imagine yourself in the scene of that rather long gospel passage from St. Mark. There is a place for each of us, since we are all paralyzed in different ways from the mystery and debilitating effects of sin at various times in our lives. Conversely, each one of us is strengthened in our faith and in our respective faith journey by the witness and faith of others. No man or woman is an island. We are not walking with the Lord Jesus by ourselves.

What an incredible scene, what a dramatic disruption of Jesus' sermon in the house near the lake of Capernaum—that little town of Capernaum, his corporate headquarters! Assume we were all packed in the living room of this house together with Jesus when suddenly debris begins to shower down on us as a human-sized hole opens in the terraced roof and a stretcher with a person strapped to it is slowly lowered. They destroyed his roof in their efforts to get to him. Today we would expect an alarm to go off during the break-in.

What was happening involved an ingenious, persistent, and bold quartet determined to bring this person, who was paralyzed, to Jesus for physical healing. There were obstacles. Scripture tells us that around the house "many gathered together so that there was no longer room for them, not even around the door" (Mk 2:2). They had to be men of deep faith. Jesus' reputation as a healer had spread throughout the region, after all. He was nothing less than a healing rock star. They were seeking to encounter Jesus. And they did.

What happened initially was certainly not what they had had in mind. Without having asked the paralytic any questions about his condition or the state of his soul, Jesus immediately diagnosed the problem and provided his remedy, made possible by five most significant and unforgettable words: "Child, your sins are forgiven" (Mk 2:5). Originally the man and his companions had sought a physical healing, but Jesus suddenly turned it into the healing of sins. Jesus was impressed by the faith of the four companions who were determined, creatively and persistently, to bring this paralyzed person to him. Having acknowledged *their* faith, he then turned to the business at hand—his business, the business he became man to accomplish and continues to accomplish in our day—the business of such healing encounters, encounters of forgiveness.

It was not until later in the story, after some of the scribes had challenged Jesus' authority to forgive sin, that he finally turned to the paralytic and said, "I say to you, rise, pick up your mat, and go home" (Mk 2:11).

Now what is at work here? It is clear that the type of healing on Jesus' *priority* list is the healing from sin, the forgiveness of sin. He *first* forgave the paralytic's sins, and only afterward did he heal the physical paralysis. In a certain way, however, St. Mark challenges us to see sin itself as a kind of paralysis, a spiritual paralysis. Such paralysis, not unlike a physical paralysis, cannot be healed without the help of someone else. A skilled doctor, with the aid of attendants who bring the person to him, heals the patient. Or in this case, the paralyzed man was brought to a healing father who was able to diagnose and heal the underlying spiritual malady, the malady of sin.

One wonders what was on the mind of the paralyzed man throughout this entire ordeal. We have no concrete evidence of what he was thinking. He said nothing. Was he even thinking of the paralysis of sin, or was he focused on his physical condition alone? So often we get understandably distracted in life with our physical ailments and forget that most underlying need for forgiveness and healing in our lives. And each of us needs the freeing experience of forgiveness.

The paralyzed man had to have known the Hebrew Psalm 51, the psalm we pray in the Liturgy of the Hours each Friday morning:

> Have mercy on me, God, in your kindness.
> In your compassion blot out my offense.
> O wash me more and more from my guilt
> and cleanse me from my sin.
> My offenses truly I know them;
> my sin is always before me.
> Against you, you alone, have I sinned;
> what is evil in your sight I have done. . . .
> A pure heart create for me, O God,
> put a steadfast spirit within me.
> Do not cast me away from your presence,
> nor deprive me of your holy spirit.

As he lay before the feet of Jesus, might the paralytic man have had that prayer on his mind? It certainly should be our prayer as we seek to encounter a forgiving and merciful God, a God who forgives us our sins and loves us beyond all telling.

As Pope Francis said in his first Sunday audience talk as pope:

> Let us not forget his word: God never tires of forgiving us! . . . Well, the problem is that we ourselves tire, we do not want to ask, we grow weary of asking for forgiveness. He never tires of forgiving, but at times we get tired of asking for forgiveness. (March 17, 2013)

At its heart, sin (a topic we do not spend much time talking about today) is a rupture of communion with God. It damages our relationship with each other in its social consequences. The *Catechism* teaches that after the first sin (i.e., original sin) the "world is virtually inundated by sin" (*CCC* 401). Even though sin is not much spoken of, you and I know—if we are truly honest with ourselves—that sin, that dark side of the human person (every human person), is a real challenge in each of our lives. And it calls out for healing, forgiveness, and a new start.

The sin might be a hatred for someone, and we fail to diagnose it as sin. It might be directing uncharitable words toward someone we work with, or a relative or family member. Gossip has a chilling effect on relationships and is sinful. It might be our failure to make Jesus the center of our lives, especially with all of the preoccupations of the modern Sunday, when we simply do not get to Mass. With all the competing sports and social events that are a part of our hectic lives today, we may fail to make Mass and family life the center of Sunday. Sunday is, after all, the Lord's day—and not ours alone.

We are called to repent and to do so regularly. In theological terms, we call repentance *metanoia*, a change of heart. And that is precisely the mission of Jesus when, in his very first words in his public ministry, he challenged those around him to "repent" and believe the Good News. This repentance or change of heart is a movement away from ourselves, with all our human challenges. It is a movement toward God.

And Jesus continues to minister in our midst, most uniquely in the person of the priest in sacramental confession.

If we examine our own lives today, we can see how it is that our narrow-mindedness, stubbornness, and unwillingness to seek forgiveness from sin and forgive others can paralyze us. This spiritual paralysis affects and afflicts our relationship with people, especially members of our families, friends, and coworkers.

We must each day ask ourselves, in the light of prayer and under the influence of the Holy Spirit, whether we are too unbending, uncooperative, unforgiving, always right and never wrong, stiff, rigid, and hardheaded. In effect, how do we sin? Moreover, are we paralyzed? Are we frozen in our sinful ways so that we fail to love and fail to put ourselves regularly and fully at the sacrificial service of each other? Each of us, no doubt, will answer that question with a yes *and* no. This exercise might be the kind of effort we adopt particularly during Lent. But whether during Lent or not, a daily examination of conscience can help us focus on our lives of sin and pray for the grace to be convicted, in particular, of that one gnawing sin that keeps us from the Lord and each other.

Then we can turn to the one who "has authority to forgive sins on earth" (Mk 2:10). In the words of Isaiah, "It is I, I, who wipe out, for my own sake, your offenses; your sins I remember no more" (Is 43:25). Or in the words of Psalm 51, we pray, "A clean heart create for me, God; renew in me a steadfast spirit. Do not drive me from your presence, nor take from me your holy spirit" (Ps 51:12–13). Forgiveness *is* a divine prerogative and priority. It is a way to encounter the healing Jesus. And it is so freeing and full of love, the love of a new start.

It is important also to realize when we read the gospel text about the paralytic that it is not always someone else on that mat or stretcher. Each of us is there. Each of us is, moreover, a prodigal son or daughter. It might be our inclination not to think of ourselves as candidates for spiritual healing and for-giveness. In truth, you and I are also paralyzed and stretched out on that mat, paralyzed by sin and in need of help, as each of us is in need of helping others find their way to the Lord—perhaps after a long time away from the faith and the Church. We are at the same time *both* in need of healing like the paralytic from St. Mark's gospel and challenged to help others as those four men who brought the paralytic to Jesus.

At the beginning of this chapter, I mentioned that three significant themes are at work in this gospel from St. Mark. The themes are evangelization, recon-ciliation, and celebration. You might ask, how is that?

First, the four men represent so beautifully and practically evangelization at work—reaching out in love to someone in need, spiritually and physically, and bringing that person to Jesus against all odds. This evangelization means being creative and at the same time persistent. Imagine working your way through the crowd of people and having the ingenu-ity to open a hole in the roof to lower a person down to Jesus! Genuine evangelization presents all kinds of challenges. The smart and persistent among us cooperate with the Lord in overcoming difficult challenges as these four men did. Why not pray daily for this specific grace of evangelization, the grace to help one person with his or her faith, one person who has been away from the sacraments, one person who has been away from the Church? Evangelization should be a way of life. And each of us has friends and acquaintances who need evangelizing. They might be family members or even close friends or neighbors. And unless we invite them to the Lord Jesus, who will? It takes risk to invite someone back to the Lord or to introduce someone to him. But such evangelization is assuredly moved by grace. And our God will never let us down as we try and do his work.

Second, with the compassionate words of forgiveness, Jesus reconciles the man in the gospel text to himself by forgiving his sins and healing his body. I speak of the continuation, in our day, of that healing ministry of Jesus. We call it the centuries-old practice of sacramental confession—the sacrament of Penance, the sacrament of Reconciliation. New York Cardinal Timothy Dolan referred to it at the Synod on the New Evangelization as the "primary sacrament of the New Evangelization."[23] Reconciliation is the sacrament of forgiveness and conversion of heart. When you pull back the velvet curtain or open the door in the reconciliation room, think of Jesus healing the paralytic at Capernaum.

The sacrament of Penance is

> a personal encounter with Jesus, the healing Je-
> sus, the same Jesus (in the person of the priest)
> who spent a great part of his life on earth heal-
> ing and forgiving. . . . The Sacrament of Pen-
> ance is extremely personal. Sins cannot be faxed,
> e-mailed, or delivered by FedEx.[24]

The sacrament of Penance is an individual encounter with Jesus, in the person of the priest, which includes a confessing of our sins, a personal act of sorrow, and an intention to amend our lives and do penance as prescribed. Could there be a more personal encounter with the crucified and forgiving Jesus, who forgave his murderers from the Cross and now forgives us in the ministry of Reconciliation with the words that our sins are forgiven and an admonition not to sin again? We cannot forget the Jesus at Capernaum who simi-larly told the paralyzed person, "Child, your sins are forgiven" (Mk 2:5).

In the words of the psalmist, we pray to the Lord, "Heal me, I have sinned against you" (Ps 41:5). For some, this encounter with Jesus is a regular part of their spiritual journeys; for others, it is not. But as our gospel text demonstrates, for each of us, the particu-lar challenge today is to bring others to this encoun-ter with Christ in that healing sacrament or bring ourselves to experience that treasure of our living faith—a forgiveness that only the Lord Jesus can give.

Finally, at the instance of the healing, celebration takes place. The gospel text tells us that "they were all astounded and glorified God, saying, 'We have never seen anything like this'" (Mk 2:12). Yes, they glorified and praised God. That is what we do every time we praise the Lord in prayer. It is our prayer of joy. From Psalm 51, we hear, "Give me again the joy of your help; with a spirit of fervor sustain me, that I may teach transgressors your ways and sinners may return to you" (Ps 51:14–15). We praise and give thanks to God for all the great things he has done and continues to do for each of us, especially the healing forgiveness of our sins. There could be no better way to give thanks to the Lord than by having an encounter with him and bringing someone else to encounter him in the healing and forgiveness of confession.

Evangelize! Reconcile! Celebrate! Each theme is linked to the other. Each brings us closer to an encounter with the Lord Jesus, and each brings us closer to one another. How wonderful our life in the Lord with each other would be if that threefold mantra took root regularly in our hearts in a new and more profound way! With God's holy grace and our free response, that can surely happen and each of us will be all the better because of this sacramental healing and forgiving encounter with Jesus. And we would then say with the psalmist in Psalm 51:16–17:

> Rescue me from death, God, my saving God,
> that my tongue may praise your healing power.
> Lord, open my lips;
> my mouth will proclaim your praise.

Reflect

Read again about the healing of the paralytic (Mark 2:1–12).

1. What are some of the ways that are available for you to become more aware of the reality of sin in your life and the need for a change of heart?

2. Who in your life provides you with the kind of help that the four friends provided to the paralytic man when they lowered him down to Jesus?

3. What keeps you from celebrating the sacrament of Penance?

4. What are some of the areas in your life that are in need of healing?

Pray

My God,
I am sorry for my sins with all my heart.
In choosing to do wrong and failing to do good,
I have sinned against you
whom I should love above all things.
I firmly intend, with your help,
to do penance, to sin no more,
and to avoid whatever leads me to sin.
Our Savior Jesus Christ suffered and died for us.
In his Name, my God, have mercy.
Amen.

SIX

The Road to Emmaus:
A Eucharistic Encounter

We come now to our encounter with Jesus in the Eucharist. The Eucharist is—as the Second Vatican Council has taught us—"the fount and apex" of the whole Christian life (*LG* 11). It is the highest form of prayer and the place *par excellence* where we may encounter the risen Christ. Or as Benedict XVI has said when speaking of the Church:

> But the place where [the Church] is fully experienced as Church is in the liturgy: it is the act in which we believe that God enters our reality and we can encounter Him, we can touch Him. It is the act in which we come into contact with God; he comes to us, and we are illuminated by him. (Audience, October 3, 2012)

We begin this chapter with the encounter of two disciples with Jesus on the road to Emmaus, narrated in the Gospel of Luke:

> Now that very day two of them were going to a village seven miles from Jerusalem called Em-

maus, and they were conversing about all the things that had occurred. And it happened that while they were conversing and debating, Jesus himself drew near and walked with them, but their eyes were prevented from recognizing him. He asked them, "What are you discussing as you walk along?" They stopped, looking downcast. One of them, named Cleopas, said to him in reply, "Are you the only visitor to Jerusalem who does not know of the things that have taken place there in these days?" And he replied to them, "What sort of things?" They said to him, "The things that happened to Jesus the Nazarene, who was a prophet mighty in deed and word before God and all the people, how our chief priests and rulers both handed him over to a sentence of death and crucified him. But we were hoping that he would be the one to redeem Israel; and besides all this, it is now the third day since this took place. Some women from our group, however, have astounded us: they were at the tomb early in the morning and did not find his body; they came back and reported that they had indeed seen a vision of angels who announced that he was alive. Then some of those with us went to the tomb and found things just as the women had described, but him they did not see." And he said to them, "Oh, how foolish you are! How slow of heart to believe all that the prophets spoke! Was it not necessary that the Messiah should suffer these things and enter into his glory?" Then beginning with Moses and all the prophets, he interpreted to them what referred to him in all the scriptures. As they approached the village to which they were going, he gave the impression that he was going on farther. But they urged him, "Stay with us, for it is nearly evening and the day is almost over." So he went in to stay with them. And it happened that, while he was with them at table, he took bread, said the blessing, broke it, and gave it to them. With that their eyes were opened and they recognized him, but he vanished from their sight. Then they said to each other, "Were not our hearts burning (within us) while he spoke to us on the way and opened the scriptures to us?" So they set out at once and returned to Jerusalem where they found gathered together the eleven and those with them who were saying, "The Lord has truly been raised and has appeared to Simon!" Then the two recounted what had taken place on the way and how he was made known to them in the breaking of the bread. (Lk 24:13–35)

You might wonder why I chose a post-resurrection gospel text for this chapter. Short answer—in the Eucharist, we encounter the risen Jesus, the Easter Jesus. The Eucharist is, moreover, the highest form of prayer. And at its heart, the Eucharist is a sharing in the life of the risen Jesus. It is a sharing in that victory won by him for us almost two thousand years ago. In fact, that is how it is possible to encounter Jesus in the Eucharist and in all the sacraments in the first place. That silent army of Catholics who regularly come to daily Mass know this truth, and it is our duty to share it.

Reflecting on that Lucan text, in his installation homily as archbishop of New York on April 15, 2009, Cardinal Dolan suggested that "we all take a little stroll down . . . the road to Emmaus." And he asked the question:

> Are we not at times perhaps like those two dejected disciples on the road to Emmaus? They were so absorbed in their own woes, so forlorn in their mistaken conclusion that the one in whom they had placed their trust was dead, so shocked by the shame, scandal, and scorn of last Friday [Good Friday] . . . that they failed to recognize Jesus [at least initially] as He walked right alongside of them! I say to you, my sister and brother disciples now on the road to Emmaus, let's not turn inward to ourselves, our worries, our burdens, our fears; but turn rather to *Him*, the way, the truth, and the life, the one who told us over and over, "Be not afraid!", who assured us that he "would be with us all days, even to the end of the world," and who promised us that "not even the gates of hell would prevail," the one who John Paul the Great called, "the answer to the question posed by every human life," and recognize him again in his word, in the "breaking of the bread," in His Church. Let Him "turn us around" as He did those two disciples, turned them around because, simply put, they were

going the wrong way, and sent them running back to Jerusalem, where Peter was, where the apostles were, where the Church was.[25]

Pope Francis likewise reflected on what occurred on the road to Emmaus in his homily on the occasion of his formal installment as bishop of Rome at the Cathedral of John Lateran:

> Let us think too of the two disciples on the way to Emmaus: their sad faces, their barren journey, their despair. But Jesus does not abandon them: he walks beside them, and not only that! Patiently he explains the Scriptures which spoke of him, and he stays to share a meal with them. This is God's way of doing things: he is not impatient like us, who often want everything all at once, even in our dealings with other people. God is patient with us because he loves us, and those who love are able to understand, to hope, to inspire confidence; they do not give up, they do not burn bridges, they are able to forgive. Let us remember this in our lives as Christians: God always waits for us, even when we have left him behind! He is never far from us, and if we return to him, he is ready to embrace us. (Homily, April 7, 2013)

And they returned to the same upper room where the Eucharist had been instituted on the Thursday night before. And the risen Jesus appeared to them upon their arrival and said, "Peace be with you." They were startled and terrified for they thought they were seeing a ghost. He encouraged them to touch his hands and feet stating that a ghost does not have flesh and bones as he did. Then he ate in front of them. They were encountering Jesus, the risen Jesus.

But they had encountered him before on that road to Emmaus both in the breaking open of the Word and the breaking of the Bread. "Luke's account of the disciples on the way to Emmaus enables us to reflect further on this link between the hearing of the word and the breaking of the bread" (*VD* 54).

This scripture passage from St. Luke, one of my favorites in all of the Bible, is akin to a paradigm of the holy Mass. I would say it helps give us a biblical basis for the two parts of the Liturgy—the Liturgy of the Word and the Liturgy of the Eucharist. And we encounter the living Christ, the Risen One, in each part of the Mass as those disciples did on the road to Emmaus and as they did when they returned to the upper room in Jerusalem.

To begin with, the Second Vatican Council makes it clear that there are *two* parts that make up each Mass. They are called the Liturgy of the Word *and* the Liturgy of the Eucharist. Although divided in two, the Council stressed that these two parts are "so closely connected with each other that they form but *one* single act of worship" (*SC* 56; emphasis added). "The Eucharistic table set for us is the table both of the Word of God and of the Body of the Lord" (*CCC* 1346).

At the beginning of the text, we read that it was the "first day of the week"—a Sunday. That is significant. It was the first Easter Sunday. We as Christians,

to help us prolong the celebration of that most fundamental mystery of our faith, to which our every hope
is pinned, celebrate Easter every Sunday. In a particular way, we celebrate Easter at Sunday Mass. Every
Sunday Mass is a mini-Easter or, in the words of St.
Augustine, "the sacrament of Easter."

What took place on that "first day of the week,"
almost two thousand years ago, St. Luke recounts for
us in that incredible post-resurrection story about two
of Jesus' disciples whose hopes had been dashed. We
can certainly picture ourselves in the same situation.
They must have been greatly disappointed as they
walked with each other "looking downcast," seeking
to console each other, for, in their own words, "we
were hoping that he would [have been] . . . the one to
redeem Israel" (Lk 24:21).

While they were walking those seven miles from
Jerusalem to the village of Emmaus, they became so
lost in their own conversation that they did not notice
the one who had joined them in their journey. He asked
them about what they were discussing. They replied
pointedly, "Are you the only visitor to Jerusalem who
does not know of the things that have taken place
there in these days?" (Lk 24:18). They explained how
Jesus had been handed over to the chief priests and
rulers to be crucified.

But in reality, and we know this truth with the eyes
of faith, Jesus Christ was not dead. He is not dead. He
has risen as he promised. It was the risen Lord who
was walking with them on that road to Emmaus, the
risen Jesus whom they encountered.

What followed in the story happens every time we gather for Mass, the Eucharistic sacrament—each day, and importantly each and every Sunday, the day of the Resurrection.

Each Sunday at Mass is an encounter with the risen Lord as the two disciples encountered him on their seven-mile walk to Emmaus on that "first day of the week," that first Easter Sunday.

So often at Mass, we too fail—at least at the outset—to acknowledge his abiding presence as they did. But at each Mass, is it not the risen Lord who breaks open the Word of God in our scripture readings through the power of the Holy Spirit? How else would his Word be the *living* Word of God if it were not he? "Then beginning with Moses and all the prophets, he interpreted to them what referred to him in all the Scriptures" (Lk 24:27). This situation is similar to the Liturgy of the Word that includes the reading of scripture and delivery of a homily reflecting on that text from scripture. That is what Jesus did. He spoke of the Old Testament figures and "interpreted to them what referred to him in all the scriptures"—not unlike a homily, the first homily. Jesus continues to do that each time we hear the scriptures read at Mass. Are we not like the two disciples? Do we not sometimes, after the Liturgy of the Word, say to ourselves, "Were not our hearts burning within us while he spoke to us . . . and opened the scriptures to us?" The Word of God has that effect. It changes us, transforms us, and fills us with his amazing grace. His presence becomes real to us in the opening up of his Word at each Mass. It is there that we encounter the living Jesus, and yet so often we forget that truth that these inspired words are the words of everlasting life. God often speaks to us, in words we most need to hear, if we truly listen. That is what it means to encounter him in his life-giving Word.

In *Verbum Domini,* Benedict XVI writes:

> And yet, apparently not even these words were enough for the two disciples. The *Gospel of Luke* relates that "their eyes were opened and they recognized him" (24:31) only when Jesus took the bread, said the blessing, broke it and gave it to them, whereas earlier "their eyes were kept from recognizing him" (24:16). . . . Now they were able to appreciate *in a new way* all that they had previously experienced with him: "Did not our hearts burn within us while he talked to us on the road, while he opened to us the Scriptures?" (24:32). (*VD* 54)

For they had urged Jesus to stay with them when they reached Emmaus. "And it happened that, while he was with them at table, he took the bread, said the blessing, broke it, and gave it to them" (Lk 24:30). St. Luke tells us that "with that their eyes were opened and they recognized him, but he vanished from their sight" (Lk 24:31). Later, they were able to tell the others back in Jerusalem "how he was made known to them in the breaking of the bread" (Lk 24:35). Does that not happen each and every time we gather for Mass? Is it not the risen Lord broken for us and poured out for us? Is it not the risen Lord who ransomed us and did so with his precious blood as if it were from a spotless, unblemished lamb? And do we not also come to recognize him, the same risen Jesus, in the breaking of the bread each time we gather for Mass and encounter him personally? He left us the Mass as a lasting memorial, and in that memorial, we are nourished. It is the only food we eat that turns us into God—what an encounter!

As if to conclude, Benedict XVI in *Verbum Domini* states that

> . . . it is clear that Scripture itself points us toward an appreciation of its own unbreakable bond with the Eucharist. "It can never be forgotten that the divine word, read and proclaimed by the Church, has as its one purpose the sacrifice of the new covenant and the banquet of grace, that is, the Eucharist." Word and Eucharist are so deeply bound together that we cannot understand one without the other: the word of God sacramentally takes flesh in the event of the Eucharist. The Eucharist opens us to an understanding of Scripture, just as Scripture for its part illumines and explains the mystery of the Eucharist. Unless we acknowledge the Lord's real presence in the Eucharist, our understanding of Scripture remains imperfect. For this reason "the Church has honored the word of God and the Eucharistic mystery with the same reverence, although not with the same worship, and has always and everywhere insisted upon and sanctioned such honor." (*VD* 55)

The Eucharist is *the* outstanding moment of encounter with the living Jesus. It is where Calvary and the Last Supper become present. It is a sacrificial meal, after all. Under the appearances of bread and wine, we truly receive the living, risen Lord Jesus. Each and every time we come to Communion, we are transformed into him. In receiving Holy Communion, we become one with him, and through him, one with each other. It is truly, really, and substantially our God. Please never forget that. I am quite sure the disciples never forgot what happened to them on the road to Emmaus and *at* Emmaus. They came to know him in the breaking of the bread, and their hearts were burning while he spoke to them and opened the scriptures to them.

In that installation homily in 2009, the then–archbishop of New York, Timothy Dolan, recounted an earlier pilgrimage to Israel. He spoke of a wonderful Franciscan guide, and he recalled a question the guide had for him the day before the cardinal was to return to the United States. The guide asked him, "Is there anything left you want to see?" Cardinal Dolan replied that he would like to walk the road to Emmaus. The guide told him that was not possible. "You see, no one really knows where that village of Emmaus actually was, so there is no more road to Emmaus." Sensing Cardinal Dolan's disappointment, he remarked, "Maybe that's part of God's providence, because we can now make *every* journey we undertake a walk down the road to Emmaus."

Cardinal Dolan concluded his homily by saying:

> My new friends of this great archdiocese, would
> you join your new pastor on an "adventure in fi-
> delity," as we turn the Staten Island Expressway,
> Fifth Avenue, Madison Avenue, Broadway, the
> FDR, the Major Deegan, and the New York State
> Thruway into the Road to Emmaus, as we wit-
> ness a real "miracle on 34th street" and turn that
> into the road to Emmaus? . . . He is walking right
> alongside us.[26]

And that is no different for you or me. Jesus is
walking with us every day of the year and each and
every moment of the day. You see, we are part of his
living body, the Church. Each time we encounter him
in his body and blood and experience his living presence in the Word of God at holy Mass, we build up
his body. It is as if we were on that road with him. In
fact, we *are* on that road with him. It is called the road
of life, and it winds through every dimension of our
lives. And there is a special stop at holy Mass because
it is there, the "fount and apex" of our Christians
lives, that we encounter him in the most profound
way. Like the two disciples who were with him on the
Emmaus road, we will be able to say over and over
again the story of the importance of "what had taken
place on the way and how he was made known to
them [and us] in the breaking of the bread" (Lk 24:35).

Reflect

Read again about the road to Emmaus (Luke 24:13–35).

1. Why do you sometimes fail to encounter Christ
    at Mass?

2. Has there been a particular time when the Word
    of God came alive for you like it did for the
    disciples on the road to Emmaus?

3. What are the moments at Sunday Eucharist when
    it is easiest for you to encounter Christ?

Pray

> O risen Christ,
> on the road to Emmaus you were the disciples'
>   companion.
> Be at our side on the journey of faith,
> on life's pathways and at every encounter;
> engender our compassion
>   so that we may welcome others
> and listen to their stories.
> Kindle anew the desire to proclaim your Word.
> May it illumine us, and may our hearts burn to bear
>   witness to it.
> May your Holy Spirit teach us the art of
>   explaining scripture
> and open our eyes to recognize you.
> Grant us the courage to become vulnerable
> so that our sisters and brothers may know you
>   through us
> and that we may know you through them.
> Amen.[27]

Part III:
Encountering Jesus
in Works of Charity

SEVEN

The Charity of the Good
Samaritan in All of Us

Having reflected on our encounter with Jesus in his Word and in the sacraments, we now turn to the third way in which we encounter Jesus—in works of charity. Benedict XVI, considering the parable of the rich young man, wrote, "As often happens in the Gospels, everything begins from an encounter" (Audience, October 14, 2012). He was speaking of the young man who "ran up, knelt down before him," and asked Jesus what he had to do to inherit eternal life (Mk 10:17). In this "encounter," he was told ultimately to sell what he had, give the proceeds to the poor, and then come and follow Jesus. Scripture does not indicate whether the rich young man followed the command of Jesus to sell and give to the poor, a supreme act of charity. But we do know that, as is often the case, this challenge began with an encounter with Jesus, an encounter in which the demand to be charitable was at the heart of God's Word.

We read in the Introduction that Benedict XVI, in his encyclical *Deus Caritas Est*, reminds us that charity is an integral dimension of the Church's ministry:

The Church's deepest nature is expressed in her three-fold responsibility: of proclaiming the word of God (*kerygma-martyria*), celebrating the sacraments (*leitourgia*), and exercising the ministry of charity (*diakonia*). These duties presuppose each other and are inseparable. For the Church, charity is not a kind of welfare activity which could equally well be left to others, but is a part of her nature, an indispensable expression of her very being. (*DCE* 25)

In his audience talk of April 25, 2012, Benedict XVI reflected on Acts 6:1–7 where the twelve apostles appoint deacons to provide for the needs of the widows. In this context Benedict reflected that from its earliest days the Church was confronted with the need to face *both* the proclamation of the Word *and* works of concrete charity:

They were facing the primary need to proclaim God's word in accordance with the Lord's mandate but—even if this was a priority of the Church—they considered with equal gravity the duty of charity and justice, that is, the duty to help widows and poor people and, in response to the commandment of Jesus: love one another as I have loved you (cf. Jn 15:12,17), to provide lovingly for their brothers and sisters in need.

So it was that difficulties arose in the two activities that must coexist in the Church—the proclamation of the word, the primacy of God and concrete charity, justice—and it was necessary to find a solution so that there would be room for both, for their necessary relationship. . . .

Since that moment a ministry of charity has existed in the Church. The Church must not only proclaim the word but must also put the word—which is charity and truth—into practice. (Audience, April 25, 2012)

In this chapter, we look at "the charity of the Good Samaritan in all of us." This well-known scripture text is found only in the Gospel of St. Luke. It is the first of two texts that we examine and that reflect an encounter with Jesus in works of charity—both in the recipient of our charity and in the actual act of charity itself.

True charity, after all, is that which opens persons to knowledge of the Great Mystery: that of the Father's love for man in Jesus Christ, found concretely in and through someone else. It enables each and every person to say credibly, with the same personal feeling of St. Paul, that Christ "has loved me and given himself up for me" (Gal 2:20). As we seek to imitate the love of Christ, which is within each of us, since Christ lives within us, we encounter him in the process. Our acts of love become acts of Christ living within us and are reflected in our actions of love. We also meet Christ Jesus in the persons we help, the "objects" (or better stated, the "subjects") of our charity.

We now reflect on the gospel story of the Good Samaritan:

There was a scholar of the law who stood up to test him and said, "Teacher, what must I do to inherit eternal life?" Jesus said to him, "What is written in the law? How do you read it?" He said in reply, "You shall love the Lord, your God, with all your heart, with all your being, with all your strength, and with all your mind, and your neighbor as yourself." He replied to him, "You have answered correctly; do this and you will live." But because he wished to justify himself, he said to Jesus, "And who is my neighbor?" Jesus replied, "A man fell victim to robbers as he went down from Jerusalem to Jericho. They stripped and beat him and went off leaving him half-dead. A priest happened to be going down that road, but when he saw him, he passed by on the opposite side. Likewise a Levite came to the place, and when he saw him, he passed by on the opposite side. But a Samaritan traveler who came upon him was moved with compassion at the sight. He approached the victim, poured oil and wine over his wounds and bandaged them. Then he lifted him up on his own animal, took him to an inn and cared for him. The next day he took out two silver coins and gave them to the innkeeper with the instruction, 'Take care of him. If you spend more than what I have given you, I shall repay you on my way back.' Which of these three, in your opinion, was neighbor to the robbers' victim?" He answered, "The one who treated him with mercy." Jesus said to him, "Go and do likewise." (Lk 10:25–37)

Today we seem to live in our cars almost as much as we live in our homes. We like to travel, to see the country. There are millions of us on the highways. Some get stuck there. Undoubtedly, you have—at some point in your life—experienced a car breaking down, a tire going flat, or an engine running out of gas, as I have. The scene is so typical—the wait for help by the side of the road with the car hood up.

Help is typically not a Samaritan, but a patrolman or perhaps a AAA employee. More often than not, we do not stop when we see someone stranded by the roadside. We keep passing. In fact, some states even have laws prohibiting stopping on the highways— even to help—because of the danger.

Or a similar situation happens to each of us who lives or works in the city. Invariably, we are confronted—often daily—with a panhandler or someone in our face seeking money as we walk to the subway or to our offices. "Custody of the eyes" is certainly one response—not even to look at the person in need. Sometimes there is a confrontation; often we look, smile maybe, and keep walking. Most of the time we do not respond. We simply walk by, justifying our behavior by thinking that we have already given to Catholic Charities, or some other charity. We convince ourselves that to give to that specific street person would probably make worse a drinking or drug habit, which that person already has. We justify noninvolvement and keep walking.

Not unlike ourselves, the Samaritan, from the passage we just read, could have easily passed by as well, and for a very special reason. There was, after all, a social taboo that forbade Samaritans from associating with Jews. Jesus himself had been refused welcome in a Samaritan village. There was a deep animosity between Jews and Samaritans. The Samaritan was risking censure and rejection by going down into that ditch to help the man who had been stripped by robbers, beaten, and left half-dead along the side of the road. But he went anyway. Such assaults were typical on the road that led from Jericho to Jerusalem. Faking injuries was a common ploy to set an ambush on that road. The Samaritan, moreover, does even more than provide simple aid. His ministrations are caring and numerous with a promise of returning on his way back to compensate the innkeeper should more money be required.

The priest and the Levite are not of the same mind. Both passed right by the injured man. The priest and the Levite were concerned about the Law and may have passed him by more out of fear than indifference. Importantly, the Law forbade them, after all, from taking part in Temple services if they had touched a corpse. They would have had to undergo elaborate cleansing ceremonies. They would have been defiled, according to the Law.

Now comes the major question of the parable: Of the three, then, who is the neighbor? This is the question that the lawyer, the scholar of the Law, that master of exegesis, posed to Jesus. It was linked to his initial concern regarding what one must do to gain eternal life. At the heart of the answer, Jesus (quoting Jewish scripture) states that in addition to loving God "with all your heart, with all your being, with all your strength, and with all your mind," you must love "your neighbor as yourself." The parable of the Good Samaritan, which followed immediately, is Jesus' answer to the lawyer's question regarding who is his neighbor.

Jesus answers the question straightaway, indicating, in fact, that the neighbor is "the one who treated him with mercy." That was the Samaritan. This had to be a shocking answer. By tradition, neighbors meant a fellow member of one's people. Seemingly, that rule was no longer operative. As Benedict XVI, in his book *Jesus of Nazareth: From the Baptism in the Jordan to the Transfiguration*, writes regarding this parable:

> It was also taken for granted that the Samaritans, who not long before (between the years A.D. 6 and 9) had defiled the Temple precincts in Jerusalem by "strewing dead men's bones" during the Passover festival itself were not neighbors. . . .
>
> But Jesus now turns the whole matter on its head: The Samaritan, the foreigner, makes himself the neighbor and shows me that I have to learn to be a neighbor deep within and that I already have the answer in myself. I have to become like someone in love, someone whose heart is open to being shaken up by another's need. Then I find my neighbor, or—better—then I am found by him.[28]

As Christians, we cannot define neighbor by law or tradition or set limits—geographical, ethnic, or religious. For us, a neighbor is not an object or a thing. The neighbor is a person.

In point of fact, I would suggest that there are two neighbors in this Lucan passage—the one in need of mercy and compassion *and* the one who acts in mercy. At its deepest sense and in a very subtle way, the neighbor is the Lord Jesus in both persons. And in all our works of charity, we encounter him in another and in ourselves.

First, Jesus is "the image of the invisible God," crying out from the man who lies half-dead and stripped on the roadside. He is the man in need. He is present in the parable from beginning to end. In effect, he is a kind of central character. He may be someone who works for us and is in need. Perhaps that person is a member of our family in trouble or the person next door who has no one to turn to but us. In that person, in our neighbor, we see the face of Christ. We meet Jesus. We encounter him. As Jesus said in the Last Judgment text in St. Matthew's gospel, "Amen, I say to you, whatever you did for one of these least brothers of mine, you did for me"(Mt 25:40). Jesus thus personally identifies himself with the hungry, the thirsty, the stranger, the immigrant, the prisoner, the ill, the homeless, and all of those on the fringe of society.

In a certain sense, then, the road from Jericho to Jerusalem represents a world of neighbors, a world of people in need whose true face, once uncovered, is the face of Christ himself. Or as Benedict XVI writes,

"The road from Jerusalem to Jericho thus turns out to be an image of human history; the half-dead man lying by the side of it is an image of humanity."[29] It is humanity with the face of Christ inviting us to meet Jesus and be changed by him.

Second, the neighbor is also the Samaritan. He is the person least likely to be defined as neighbor in this passage from St. Luke. Yet the Samaritan is the neighbor. A neighbor is often found in the most unlikely places.

In that same book, titled *Jesus of Nazareth: From the Baptism in the Jordan to the Transfiguration*, Benedict XVI, writing about this parable, compared the Samaritan to Christ: "God, though so remote from us, has made himself our neighbor in Jesus Christ. He pours oil and wine into our wounds, a gesture seen as an image of the healing gift of the sacraments, and he brings us to the inn."[30] Food, by analogy, is the food of life for which we come each Sunday to the inn called our parish church.

As long as Jesus lives, our neighbor is present both in the one in need and the one who serves. As St. Paul tells us, Christ Jesus "is the image of the invisible God" (Col 1:15). No longer is he invisible, but he is real and present. Even Moses knew that the Lord is "very near to you, already in your mouths and in your hearts" (Dt 30:14).

Like the Samaritan, the unexpected "neighbor," each one of us, as a follower of Jesus, is called to be a neighbor to others. Each one of us is challenged to be available, not indifferently passing by those in our way, but cultivating a sensitivity of heart that reaches out and bears witness in compassion in countless practical ways. You know our neighbors as well as I do. They are the suffering people in our lives. They live in our homes and in our families. They are our extended families at work and in the community.

Jesus was quite clear in the parable. He held up the Samaritan as a model. He told the scholar of the Law—who raised the issue of who the neighbor is— to "go and do likewise."

If we do as the Samaritan did, Jesus will unexpectedly appear to us and will reveal himself. He will give us an experience even now of the transforming joy in store for us for all eternity. We will encounter him precisely in our works of charity. For the object of our charity is a person, and that person is Jesus. He will surprise us as he did the lawyer with a parable that can and should become our way of life.

As you and I actively and concretely try to be a neighbor, as we "go and do likewise," we will also encounter unexpectedly a neighbor—a good friend named Jesus. Yes, he is Jesus, the one who lives within us; and he is the Jesus we meet in the person of the neighbor, the recipient of our charity and love. May we generously bring joy to those in need and help one another find Jesus in helping them.

A Postscript:
St. Luke's account of Mary's visitation, the second Joyful Mystery of the Rosary, speaks compellingly and beautifully to our theme in this chapter. It is the theme of encountering Jesus in works of charity.

We read that "Mary set out and travelled to the hill country *in haste* to a town of Judah, where she entered the house of Zechariah and greeted Elizabeth," her kinswoman (Lk 1:39–40; emphasis added). Mary was with child. She was with Jesus. But she remained to assist Elizabeth, who was also with child, as St. Luke tells us, for "about three months" (Lk 1:56).

At its deepest level, Mary's visitation is a true and compelling witness to the world in this age and in every age that love for one another really matters. It reminds us poignantly of our duty, as followers of Jesus, to reach out and help those in need. It was a genuine visitation of charity and love. It also under-scores the urgency of the call to charity. Scripture tells us that Mary had set out "in haste." Mary encountered Jesus in her work of charity, in the assistance she had given to her kinswoman Elizabeth while she was carrying Jesus.

So often, charity demands a ready and timely response or initiative. Mary gives us a wonderful example of the urgency of our works of charity in so many different situations. I suggest that a certain urgency is integral to all our works of charity. It is part and parcel of the loving sacrifice that charity always entails.

As we pray to our Blessed Mother, we pray that our visitations to those in need, in whatever form these visitations may take, may be filled with that same sense of loving urgency that she so beautifully modeled for all times.

Reflect

Read again about the parable of the Good Samaritan
(Luke 10:25–37).

1. What inhibits you from reaching out to others
   in need?

2. Who in your life is in need of your care this day?

Pray

> God of love, give us a deep love for you, so that
>   we can see the world as you see it, feel the
>   compassion you feel, and be a people whose
>   lives mediate your love to others.
> So open our eyes that we might see what the Good
>   Samaritan saw. Grant us the insight to see the
>   need in others, the wisdom to know what to do,
>   and the will to do it.
> And so we pray for all those who, in many and
>   various ways, have been stripped, beaten,
>   and left for dead.
> We pray for children who must grow up in the
>   most awful of circumstances, especially for
>   those starved of love, or food, or shelter, or
>   security. May they receive the future you have
>   planned for them.[31]

EIGHT

In Anticipation of the Final Judgment

To encounter Jesus is to come to know and love him and to love him in each and every one of us created in his image and likeness. This is the essential reason why we are continually challenged as a society to protect life, human life, in all forms and from conception until natural death. This is *the* continuing and underlying moral challenge in our day.

In *Deus Caritas Est,* Benedict XVI wrote about the parable of the Good Samaritan, a parable discussing the question, "Who is my neighbor?" He wrote that this Lucan parable

> ... offers two particularly important clarifications. Until that time, the concept of "neighbor" was understood as referring essentially to one's countrymen and to foreigners who had settled in the land of Israel; in other words, to the closely-knit community of a single country or people. This limit is now abolished. Anyone who needs me, and whom I can help, is my neighbor. The concept of "neighbor" is now universalized, yet it remains concrete. Despite being extended to all mankind, it is not reduced to a generic, abstract

and undemanding expression of love, but calls for my own practical commitment here and now. (*DCE* 15)

In effect, a neighbor is one in need no matter his or her background or ethnic origin. We saw in the last chapter that the neighbor in this instructive parable is both the Samaritan and the one in need. At its deepest level and in a subtle way, the neighbor is the Lord Jesus in both persons. And in our works of charity, we encounter him in one another and in ourselves.

We turn now to the well-known text from Matthew 25:31–46, a text used in year A of the *Lectionary* on the Solemnity of Our Lord Jesus Christ, the King of the Universe, which is the last Sunday of the liturgical year, the last Sunday before Advent. Benedict XVI also refers to this parable in *Deus Caritas Est*. He writes that in the parable of the Final (or Last) Judgment,

Love becomes the criterion for the definitive decision about a human life's worth or lack thereof. Jesus identifies himself with those in need, with the hungry, the thirsty, the stranger, the naked, the sick and those in prison. "As you did it to one of the least of these my brethren, you did it to me" (Mt 25:40). Love of God and love of neighbor have become one: in the least of the brethren we find Jesus himself, and in Jesus we find God. (*DCE* 15)

This parable, a parable linked to the way we will be judged on the last day, further expands the parable of the Good Samaritan and explicitly identifies the poor with the face of Jesus. This parable shows us an opportunity to encounter Jesus. In loving a neighbor in need, we love God.

Citing 1 John 4:20, "If anyone says, 'I love God,' and hates his brother, he is a liar; for he who does not love his brother whom he has seen, cannot love God whom he has not seen," Benedict XVI states furthermore that these revealed words "should rather be interpreted to mean that love of neighbor is a path that leads to the encounter with God, and that closing our eyes to our neighbor also blinds us to God" (*DCE* 16). In our works of charity, we thus see and encounter God.

> When the Son of Man comes in his glory, and all the angels with him, he will sit upon his glorious throne, and all the nations will be assembled before him. And he will separate them one from another, as a shepherd separates the sheep from the goats. He will place the sheep on his right and the goats on his left. Then the king will say to those on his right, "Come, you who are blessed by my Father. Inherit the kingdom prepared for you from the foundation of the world. For I was hungry and you gave me food, I was thirsty and you gave me drink, a stranger and you welcomed me, naked and you clothed me, ill and you cared for me, in prison and you visited me." Then the righteous will answer him and say, "Lord, when did we see you hungry and feed you, or thirsty and give you drink? When did we see you a stranger and welcome you, or naked

and clothe you? When did we see you ill or in prison, and visit you?" And the king will say to them in reply, "Amen, I say to you, whatever you did for one of these least brothers of mine, you did for me." Then he will say to those on his left, "Depart from me, you accursed, into the eternal fire prepared for the devil and his angels. For I was hungry and you gave me no food, I was thirsty and you gave me no drink, a stranger and you gave me no welcome, naked and you gave me no clothing, ill and in prison, and you did not care for me." Then they will answer and say, "Lord, when did we see you hungry or thirsty or a stranger or naked or ill or in prison, and not minister to your needs?" He will answer them, "I say to you, what you did not do for one of these least ones, you did not do for me." And these will go off to eternal punishment, but the righteous to eternal life. (Mt 25:31–46)

This parable describes how the Son of Man will come "and all the nations will be assembled before him. And he will separate them one from another, as a shepherd separates the sheep from the goats. He will place the sheep on his right and the goats on his left" (Mt 25:32–33).

This text is not simply the familiar story of the Son of Man's separation of the sheep from the goats, a foreshadowing of the final judgment, a judgment so magnificently portrayed by Michelangelo in the Sistine Chapel. It is what we profess every Sunday at Mass in the Nicene Creed when we pray, "He will come again in glory to judge the living and the dead, and his kingdom will have no end." It is about rewards and eternal punishment.

Importantly and uniquely, in this parable, Jesus is a king, and that is the reason that the parable is read on the Solemnity of Christ the King. He is a king who actually identifies himself with the weak and the weary. Specifically, he identifies with you and me. In St. Matthew's gospel parable, the king does not talk about "those" and "them" as if there existed a difference and distance between himself—the king—and those who are hungry, thirsty, strangers, naked, ill, and in prison. There is no gap between Jesus, our king, and those in need. To serve and love them is, in fact, to serve and love him. He makes that crystal clear when he says, "*I* was hungry . . . *I* was thirsty . . . *I* was a stranger . . . *I* was naked . . . *I* was ill . . . *I* was in prison." Only in such solidarity is he king. And in case we fail to grasp Jesus' appropriation of the pronoun "I" to refer to himself, he is even more specific: "Whatever you did for one of these least brothers of mine, you did for me" (Mt 25:40).

Each of us will someday be examined by the judge, by Christ, our king. We must, therefore, ponder this profound truth of our faith each and every day. For precisely in the most miserable person, we have already met our judge; and in that person we encounter Jesus. As the title of this chapter states, we encounter Jesus in anticipation of the final judgment. And that happens, or should or can happen, each and every day of our lives.

Now there is another important point in this parable. When we speak of the hungry, the thirsty, the naked, the ill, and the imprisoned, we cannot leave ourselves out of the picture. Jesus actually and concretely identifies with us precisely where we are—here and now. God reigns within us. When we pray each day the Our Father—"thy kingdom come"—we are praying that Jesus will take root anew within us. That is the kind of king Jesus is—the "first fruits of those who have fallen asleep" (1 Cor 15:20) living within us, thrilling through our very bones.

Jesus' kingdom does not have geographical limits. It is the place where Jesus is here and now. His kingdom is within each and every one of us.

In *our* hunger for him, for his abiding consolation, in our hunger for love and understanding, for respect, for dignity as persons who are unique and unrepeatable, Jesus is there. It is there that we encounter him.

In *our* thirst for the truth about our life-giving faith, authenticity, and genuine freedom, Jesus is there, and we encounter him.

In *our* nakedness, to ourselves—in those rare and pristine moments when we see ourselves as we truly are, without camouflage and without guard—Jesus is there, and we encounter him.

In *our* illness, in our fervor for Christ, in our daily brokenness, and in our woundedness, there is Jesus, and we encounter him.

Finally, in *our* prisons, the prisons of our addictions in which we so often live and the many forms of captivity that keep us in bondage, Jesus is there to free us, and we encounter him.

Thus Jesus reigns not only within each one of us as baptized Christians, as parts of his living body on earth; but also he reigns in others—the others of our lives: members of our families, our neighbors, those with whom we work and live.

Not only are *we* hungry. Others are hungry as well. And we meet Jesus in them when we feed them. Not only are *we* thirsty, thirsty for the truth; so are others. And we meet Jesus in them when we give them a drink. Not only are *we* strangers in this global village, but so are others; and we meet Jesus in them when we show kindness and hospitality. Not only are *we* naked, ill, and imprisoned; so are others. And we meet Jesus in them when we clothe, care for, and help liberate them. There is a solidarity in our world, and his solidarity with each of us is the way we come to know and love him and gain our own salvation. "Whatever you did for one of these least brothers of mine, you did for me" (Mt 25:40).

In *Deus Caritas Est*, Benedict XVI is so clear that the work of charity must continue on in the Church, not just in our individual encounters with the poor and needy, but in the institution. Such works of charity continue on in the numerous Church organizations specifically structured for charitable and philanthropic purposes. About the motivating love for such work, Benedict XVI wrote further:

> This love does not simply offer people material help, but refreshment and care for their souls,

something which often is even more necessary than material support. In the end, the claim that just social structures would make works of charity superfluous masks a materialist conception of man: the mistaken notion that man can live "by bread alone" (Mt 4:4; cf. Dt 8:3)—a conviction that demeans man and ultimately disregards all that is specifically human. (*DCE* 28)

Instead, Benedict XVI spoke of the new forms of charitable activities arising from the Church and ecclesial communities, and he sees in these new efforts the possibility "to establish a fruitful link between evangelization and works of charity" (*DCE* 30). Yes, in our works of charity, we encounter Christ.

At the same time, there are some in our nation today who would have the Church get out of the works of organized charity altogether and would even go so far as to limit our freedom to serve the poor and needy. In effect, that would restrict our opportunity to encounter Christ in them if we were restricted or prohibited in our organized efforts to serve them. Such efforts would condition our religious freedom with undue burden or restrict our freedom of conscience given by the traditional and long-standing protection of the First Amendment.

In his opening homily commencing his ministry as archbishop of Baltimore, Archbishop William Lori perceptively said:

We defend religious liberty because we are lovers of every human person, seeing in the face of every man and woman also the face of Christ, who loved us to the very end and who calls on us to love and serve our neighbor with the same love he has bestowed on us. We uphold religious liberty because we seek to continue serving those in need while contributing to the common good in accord with the Church's social teaching and to do so with compassion and effectiveness through Catholic Charities.[32]

I would add that we do so, as well, in response to Jesus' mandate: "Whatever you did for one of these least brothers of mine, you did for me" (Mt 25:40). Our salvation hangs on our response. Yes, this is the way we encounter Jesus in anticipation of the final judgment.

To some at that final judgment, those on his left, Jesus will say:

"Depart from me, you accursed, into the eternal fire prepared for the devil and his angels. For I was hungry and you gave me no food, I was thirsty and you gave me no drink, a stranger and you gave me no welcome, naked and you gave me no clothing, ill and in prison, and you did not care for me. . . . I say to you, what you did not do for one of these least ones, you did not do for me." And these will go off to eternal punishment, but the righteous to eternal life. (Mt 25:41–46)

A Postscript:

When we speak of love in a Christian context, it is a love that reflects Jesus' own heart pierced on the Cross, a love that is poured into our hearts by his Holy Spirit. It is a love that deeply cares for us when we are lost and in need every day of our lives. It is a love that takes risks for us on sunny days and on rainy days as well. It is another name for Jesus.

For Jesus is a God who continually invites us to come to him. He invites each of us who labors and is burdened from time to time. He promises rest, rest in him, and rest by his most Sacred Heart. "Take my yoke upon you and learn from me, for I am meek and humble of heart; and you will find rest for yourselves. For my yoke is easy, and my burden light" (Mt 11:29–30).

Oh what a wondrous God we have! His kindness is everlasting. It is good to pause and contemplate this fundamental truth of our faith: the unconditional love of Jesus for us. As we end this chapter, we pray, O Sacred Heart of Jesus, pray for us!

Reflect

Read again the parable of the Last Judgment (Matthew 25:31–46).

1. Who are the least of Jesus' brothers and sisters that you meet each day? Why can it be difficult to see Jesus in them?

2. In which dimensions of your life are you too one of the least of Jesus' brothers or sisters? What is your hunger or thirst? Your nakedness or imprisonment? Where are you broken or wounded?

3. How can you become more like Jesus when you perform an act of charity?

Pray

Offer this prayer from a place of need within yourself and united with the least of Jesus' brothers and sisters:

> For this reason I kneel before the Father,
> from whom every family in heaven and on earth is
>   named,
> that he may grant you in accord with the riches of
>   his glory
> to be strengthened with power through his Spirit in
>   the inner self
> and that Christ may dwell in your hearts through
>   faith;
> that you, rooted and grounded in love,

may have strength to comprehend with all the holy
    ones
what is the breadth and length and height and
    depth,
and to know the love of Christ that surpasses
    knowledge,
so that you may be filled with all the fullness of
    God.
Now to him who is able to accomplish
far more than all we ask or imagine,
by the power at work within us,
to him be glory in the church
and in Christ Jesus to all generations,
forever and ever. Amen. (Eph 3:14–21)

Abbreviations

These documents, along with the Holy Father's audiences, addresses, homilies, etc., referenced in the text, may be accessed on the Vatican's website: www.vatican.va. For materials authored by Benedict XVI, or Pope Francis, search by the type of statement and its date (e.g., "Homily"). For other texts, use the search function and search by date.

CCC   *Catechism of the Catholic Church.* Libreria Editrice Vaticana, 1997.

DCE   *God Is Love (Deus Caritas Est).* Encyclical of Benedict XVI, 2006.

EV   *The Gospel of Life (Evangelium Vitae).* Encyclical of John Paul II, 1995.

LG   *Dogmatic Constitution on the Church (Lumen Gentium).* Vatican II, 1964.

PF   *The Door of Faith (Porta Fidei).* Apostolic Letter of Benedict XVI, October 17, 2011.

RM   *Mother of the Redeemer (Redemptoris Mater).* Encyclical of John Paul II, 1987.

SC   *Constitution on the Sacred Liturgy (Sacrosanctam Concilium).* Vatican II, 1963.

USCCA   *The United States Catholic Catechism for Adults.* United States Conference of Catholic Bishops, 2006.

VD   *The Word of the Lord (Verbum Domini).* Post-Synodal Apostolic Exhortation of Benedict XVI, 2011.

Notes

1. Interview of the Holy Father Benedict XVI with Journalists during the Flight to Berlin, September 12, 2011, http://www.vatican.va/holy_father/benedict_xvi/speeches/2011/september/documents/hf_ben-xvi_spe_20110922_intervista-germania_en.html.

2. Donald W. Wuerl, "Report at the Synod of Bishops," *Zenit*, October 9, 2012, www.zenit.org/article-35675?1=english.

3. Carlo M. Martini, *Ministers of the Gospel* (Middlegreen, Slough, England: St. Paul Publications, 1983), 73.

4. John Paul II, *Crossing the Threshold of Hope* (New York: Alfred A. Knopf, 1994), 218.

5. Benedict XVI, "Address to the Carthusian Monks," *Zenit*, October 11, 2011, www.zenit.org/article-33639?1=english.

6. Benedict XVI, "Address," October 15, 2011, www.vatican.va/holy_father/ benedict_xvi/speeches/2011/october/documents/hf_ben-xvi_spe_20111015_nuova-evangelizzazione_en.html.

7. William Barclay, *The Gospel of Matthew*, vol. 2 (Westminster: John Knox Press, 1965), 61.

8. This is the refrain to the Responsorial Psalm (Psalm 65) on the Fifteenth Sunday of Ordinary Time, Year A (see Lk 8:8).

9. United States Conference of Catholic Bishops, "Prayer for the New Evangelization," www.usccb.org/

prayer-and-worship/prayers/new-evangelization-prayer.cfm.

10. Theological-Historical Commission of the Great Jubilee of the Year 2000, *Jesus Christ, Word of the Father: The Savior of the World,* trans. Adrian Walker (New York: Crossroad Publishing, 1997), 19.

11. Ibid., 21.

12. St. Ignatius, *The Spiritual Exercises of St. Ignatius* (Whitefish, MT: Kessinger Publishing, 2005), 142.

13. Incognito Magnus, *Manresa: Or the Spiritual Exercises of St. Ignatius* (London: Burns and Oats, 1881), 143.

14. Ibid., 144.

15. Anthony Lickteig, "Creed," in bulletin of Church of the Little Flower, Bethesda, MD, November 23, 2011, http://www.lfparish.org/parish/news-detail/index.aspx?linkid=52&moduleid=21.

16. St. Maximus of Turin, "Sermo 100, de sancta Epiphania 1, 3," in *Liturgy of the Hours,* The Office of Readings, Friday after Epiphany.

17. "Pope Visits Site of Jesus' Baptism in Jordan," *Rome Reports,* May 10, 2009, http://www.romereports.com/palio/pope-visits-site-of-jesus-baptism-in-jordan-english-589.html.

18. Benedict XVI, *Jesus of Nazareth: From the Baptism in the Jordan to the Transfiguration* (New York: Doubleday, 2007), 18.

19. Ibid., 23.

20. St. Leo the Great, "Sermo 1, in *Nativitate Domini*, 1–3 (PL 54, 190–193)," in *Liturgy of the Hours*, The Office of Readings, Christmas.

21. Donald W. Wuerl, "Report at the Synod of Bishops," *Zenit*, October 9, 2012, www.zenit.org/article-35675?1=english.

22. "Opening Prayer for the Baptism of the Lord," in *The Sacramentary*, 1973.

23. "Cardinal Dolan: Confession is the Sacrament of the New Evangelization," *Catholic News Agency*, October 9, 2012, http://www.catholicnewsagency.com/news/cardinal-dolan-confession-is-the-sacrament-of-new-evangelization/.

24. Peter J. Vaghi, *The Sacraments We Celebrate* (Notre Dame, IN: Ave Maria Press, 2010), 87.

25. Timothy Dolan, "Homily," Archdiocese of New York, April 15, 2009, www.archny.org/news-presss-releases/?i=12039.

26. Ibid.

27. National Council of Churches in Australia, "Opening Prayer," in Ecumenical Worship Service, 2010, www.ncca.org.au/files/. . ./Faith. . ./ 2010_Ecumenical_Worship_Service.pdf.

28. Benedict XVI, *Jesus of Nazareth: From the Baptism in the Jordan to the Transfiguration*, (New York: Doubleday, 2007), 196–97.

29. Ibid., 200.

30. Ibid., 200–201.

31. The Baptist Union of Great Britain, "Prayer: The Good Samaritan," *The Baptist Times*, July 5, 2012, www.baptisttimes.co.uk/index.php/prayer?start=10.

32. William E. Lori, "Installation Homily," Archdiocese of Baltimore, May 16, 2012, www.archbalt.org/about-us/the-archbishop/homilies/installation-homily.cfm.

Msgr. Peter J. Vaghi is pastor of the Church of the Little Flower in Bethesda, Maryland, and a priest of the Archdiocese of Washington. He received seminary and theological training at the Pontifical North American College and Gregorian University, both in Rome. Also a graduate of University of Virginia Law School, Vaghi practiced law for many years and is a member of the Virginia State Bar and the District of Columbia Bar. Vaghi serves as chaplain of the John Carroll Society, a group of professional men and women in service of the Archbishop of Washington. He is the author of the Pillars of Faith series—*The Faith We Profess, The Sacraments We Celebrate, The Commandments We Keep,* and *The Prayer We Offer*—and has written a number of articles for *America, Priest,* and *Our Sunday Visitor.* He has also contributed to two collections of writings on priestly spirituality: *Behold Your Mother* and *Born of the Eucharist.*